The third edition of this valuable book by Chris Nobes highlights the continuing importance of international classification in accounting even in a world where International Financial Reporting Standards (IFRS) are growing in importance. Nobes demonstrates comprehensively how we can use international classification schemes to better understand continuing variations in national systems as well as the different extents and also ways IFRS has been adopted and implemented.

Sid Gray, *Professor, University of Sydney, Australia*

Classifications are invaluable aids in research as well as in teaching. That applies to international accounting as much as to languages, legal systems, biology and many other disciplines. This new edition provides a much needed update on Christopher Nobes' work on the classification of financial reporting systems for a time when IFRS have been internationally widely implemented but, for many reasons outlined in this book, financial reporting continues to differ internationally.

Lisa Evans, *Professor, University of Stirling, UK*

Drawing on his extensive knowledge in accounting as well as other subjects – history, natural sciences, humanities and social sciences – Professor Nobes turns the art of classification into a tool for seeing the accounting discipline in a wider perspective.

Erlend Kvaal, *Professor, BI Norwegian Business School, Norway*

T0293494

International Classification of Financial Reporting

Financial reporting practices differ widely between countries and this has far-reaching implications for multinational businesses. Over more than a century, there have been attempts to classify countries into groups by similarities of practices. With the recent spread of International Financial Reporting Standards, it might appear that classification is largely of historical interest, but this is not the case, for several reasons explained in this book.

Christopher Nobes offers a critical analysis of the many previous accounting classifications, having drawn lessons from other fields of science and social science. Revised and updated to reflect the IFRS era, the book discusses how old classifications are reflected in today's international differences in practice under IFRS. It concludes with a discussion on the most useful classifications, and how classifications can still be relevant in the era of international standards.

This book will be essential for academics, postgraduates and undergraduates in international accounting, accounting theory and to international accounting professionals.

Christopher Nobes is Professor of Accounting at Royal Holloway (University of London) and the University of Sydney. He was a member of the Board of the International Accounting Standards Committee from 1993 to 2001. He has been a consultant to PricewaterhouseCoopers since 1987. He has been joint editor of *Accounting and Business Research*, and is now on the editorial boards of nine journals, including *Abacus*, *Accounting and Business Research* and *British Accounting Review*. He was chosen for the Outstanding International Accounting Educator Award of the American Accounting Association in 2002.

Routledge studies in accounting

International Classification of Financial Reporting

Third edition

Christopher Nobes

LONDON AND NEW YORK

First edition published 1984
by Croom Helm Ltd

Third edition published 2014
by Routledge
2 Park Square, Milton Park, Abingdon, Oxon OX14 4RN

and by Routledge
711 Third Avenue, New York, NY 10017

First issued in paperback 2017

Routledge is an imprint of the Taylor & Francis Group, an informa business

British Library Cataloguing in Publication Data
A catalogue record for this book is available from the British Library

Library of Congress Cataloging in Publication Data
Nobes, Christopher.
   International classification of financial reporting/Christopher Nobes. –
   3rd edition.
   pages cm
   Includes bibliographical references and index.
   1. Comparative accounting–Classification. 2. Financial statements.
   I. Title.
   HF5625.N63 2014
   657'.3012–dc23
                                           2013050185

ISBN 13: 978-1-138-49734-4 (pbk)
ISBN 13: 978-0-415-73693-0 (hbk)

Typeset in Times New Roman
by Wearset Ltd, Boldon, Tyne and Wear

Contents

Figures

Tables

Preface to the first edition

In late 1975, a few months after I had arrived at the University of Exeter to take up my first academic post, I decided to try to make comparative international accounting my special area of interest. My colleague, Pat Kirkman, suggested that I write for advice to Professor R.H. Parker of the University of Dundee. That I had never heard that name before is a clear demonstration of how unsullied my practising accountant's mind was with things academic. A few months later, it became clear that this man was to be the first professor of accountancy at the University of Exeter. The muses had looked down upon me with an unusually broad smile, and dealt me a stroke of such good luck that I will likely never recover from it.

I here acknowledge that this work owes much to the guidance and encouragement of Bob Parker, both in the germination of ideas over several years and during the writing. I have also benefitted greatly from the statistical and computer processing skills of John Matatko, Sue King and Bernard Pearson. John Matatko suggested the programs used, and helped to explain the results reported, on p. 69. Bernard Pearson provided the programs shown on pp. 71 and 80. Sue King turned my data into a suitable meal for the machine, and made sure that it obeyed our instructions.

I am also very grateful to Paul Rutteman of Arthur Young and Co. for putting me in contact with members of his firm's offices in six European countries. I received great assistance in those offices in April and May 1981. I also acknowledge the many useful comments of Dr Ian Stewart of the University of Auckland and Professor Sid Gray of the University of Glasgow on earlier drafts.

The persons who carried out one of the most onerous tasks were Mrs Elvy Ibbotson and Miss Susanne Robertson who typed many drafts of this work. For this I record hearty thanks.

This book is a substantial extract from my PhD thesis of 1982.

Christopher Nobes
University of Strathclyde
July 1983

Preface to the second edition

Much has changed since the first edition of this book in July 1983. In the European Community (EC) the Fourth and Seventh Directives have been implemented in most countries. Spain and Portugal have joined the EC. The IASC has issued several more standards and has become a more powerful body. The standard-setting authorities in the UK and in Australia have changed. Globalization of the securities markets has continued. The Big-9 have become the Big-6, although they are still commonly referred to as the Big-8. Several papers have been published in the area of harmonization and classification. Further useful comments have been made on my classification scheme. All of this has led to the need to amend the first edition, although some material has been left unaltered where appropriate.

Whereas the first edition was prepared and processed in Exeter and Strathclyde Universities, this one was worked on in Sydney and Reading Universities.

Christopher Nobes

Preface to the third edition

The second edition of this book was written during the academic year 1990/91. No companies of any economic importance were then using international accounting standards, whereas International Financial Reporting Standards (IFRS) are now required in about 90 countries at least for the consolidated financial statements of listed companies. Only in a few countries is IFRS not allowed, e.g. Iran, North Korea and the United States (the axis of evil?). This raises the question whether international classification of accounting has become of purely historical interest. Fortunately for this book, the answer is 'no' for several reasons, including that most accounting in most countries still uses national rules and that there are now more things to classify, such as (i) the different ways in which jurisdictions have adopted or adapted IFRS into their regulations, and (ii) the national versions of IFRS practices.

In the academic field, there has been a steady stream of papers in good journals which are directly concerned with classification.

This all justifies the production of a third edition. I am grateful to Routledge and especially to the editor, Terry Clague, for suggesting the idea and for help along the way. This edition is much larger than the second. Chapters 1 to 6 are loosely based on the previous edition, but greatly expanded. Chapters 7 and 8 are entirely new.

This book is drawn from my PhD thesis and from a large number of my publications on classification, dating from 1981 onwards, whose details are shown in the References at the end of the book. For two of those publications, I had co-authors, Stephen Zeff and Christian Stadler, respectively. I am grateful to them for all their help.

Christopher Nobes
Royal Holloway (University of London)
and University of Sydney
January 2014

1 Introduction

1.1 The importance of classification

To classify is human.

(Bowker and Star, 2000, p. 1)

Classification is a fundamental part of many disciplines. The classifications of diseases and books are vital in the daily tasks of medics and librarians, respectively. The Linnaean and Mendeleev classifications are central to learning and research in biology and chemistry. Classifications have also been made in many other fields; for example, languages (Ruhlen, 1991), economies (Neuberger and Duffy, 1976), political systems (Shils, 1966) and legal systems (David and Brierley, 1985). Some of these classifications will be examined in Chapter 2.

The everyday work of accountants involves recording transactions in the classification system that is double-entry bookkeeping. The financial statements which result are also classifications: for example, assets are classed as non-current or current; the former are then subclassed as tangible, intangible or financial. The classifications are debatable: in the income statement, should expenses be classified by nature or by function? Some classifications are metaphysical: the split of equity financial assets into trading or available-for-sale rests[1] not on any observable characteristic, or even on the real intentions of managers, but on the *declared* intentions of managers.

Classification has also been applied in the field of international accounting differences. Just as in other fields, classification has been used to assist understanding of how the many different objects (in this case, accounting systems) are related. I use the term 'accounting system' to refer to a set of accounting practices in financial statements. For example, each individual listed company in the USA has its own accounting practices. However, the accounting of all the companies has many shared characteristics, imposed and enforced by the Securities and Exchange Commission. The individual examples of US accounting share so much in common that they could be said to comprise a 'system': US GAAP (generally accepted accounting principles). Another precise, but quite different, system is French GAAP as used for unconsolidated financial statements in France. A country can exhibit more than one system. For example, although

French GAAP is still used for unconsolidated financial statements in France, the consolidated statements of French listed companies are now prepared using International Financial Reporting Standards (IFRS).

The US and French 'systems' contain few overt[2] options. However, partly as a result of international political negotiations (Camfferman and Zeff, 2007, ch. 5), many options were included in IFRS; although these are gradually being removed. When considering these options, a firm is subject to national pressures (including such matters as tax and legal systems) which make it choose differently depending on its domicile. Ball (2006, p. 15) explains how, even if all entities are complying with IFRS, the incentives of preparers and enforcers remain 'primarily local'. As a result, one can discern national patterns of IFRS practice (Kvaal and Nobes, 2010). These could be seen as different 'systems' of generic IFRS. I classify such systems in the empirical chapters of this book.

A proper understanding of accounting classifications is important for several reasons. Hundreds[3] of academic papers refer to the classifications as part of motivating research (Gray, 1988; Ball *et al.*, 2000; O'Donnell and Prather-Kinsey, 2010) or to justify an independent variable (type of accounting system) which is expected to influence issues such as value relevance (e.g. Ali and Hwang, 2000). If the classifications are inappropriate, the research setting or the variables will be questionable. For financial analysts, students and policy makers, the classifications are a convenient way of simplifying and summarising. So, again, inappropriate classifications are likely to be misleading. For instance, much of the argumentation on the development of new standards is political (Harrison and McKinnon, 1986), and is now often expressed in terms of resisting 'Anglo-American' accounting. As an example, German writers have seen the international standard-setters as a Trojan horse which conceals Anglo-American accounting (Kleekämper, 2000) or as 'the unknown enemy from London'[4] (Hennes and Metzger, 2010). Botzem and Quack (2009) believe that the history of the International Accounting Standards Committee has been wrongly reported as 'an Anglo-American success story' (p. 991). However, as will be shown, some classifiers deny the existence of Anglo-American accounting.

1.2 Outline of this book

Chapter 2 examines classifications across a wide range of disciplines and across many centuries. Lessons are collated for later use in the field of international accounting.

Chapter 3 looks at the objects of international accounting classifications: countries or 'systems' of accounting. The chapter investigates why and how accounting is different between countries, noting that (since the last edition of this book) it has become common for more than one accounting system to be used within a single country. There is also considerable variety in the practice of IFRS, along national lines, such that there are several 'systems' of IFRS, which can be classified.

Chapter 4 surveys the large number of international accounting classifications that have been drawn up over more than a century. These classifications can themselves be classified, particularly into those based on influences on accounting (extrinsic or deductive classifications) and those based on the rules or practices of financial reporting (intrinsic or inductive classifications). There is also great variation in the number of countries covered and the type of data used. Chapters 5 and 6 look in more detail at the extrinsic and intrinsic classifications, respectively, up to the end of the 1990s when international standards became important.

Chapter 7 examines the new world of IFRS. Far from rendering international accounting classifications obsolete, there are now more things to classify, especially (i) how jurisdictions have reacted to IFRS, and (ii) the several national 'systems' of IFRS practices.

Chapter 8 draws on the lessons learnt from other fields, as in Chapter 2, to ask whether the accounting classifications can be relied upon. Are they too dependent on the classifiers and the data chosen? The chapter uses data on IFRS practice to investigate the sensitivity of classification to variations in the countries and sectors included and variations in the characteristics used to measure the accounting systems.

Four appendices contain more detail on aspects of various chapters. The References list provides the details of the publications referred to in the text.

Notes

1 As under IAS 39, para. 9.
2 As explained later, I use this term to describe policy options that have been deliberately and explicitly inserted into accounting rules.
3 As examples, Nair and Frank (1980) Table 1 has 228 citations and Nobes (1983b) has 390 (according to Google Scholar, accessed on 15 April 2013).
4 'Der unbekannte Feind aus London'.

2 The purposes and processes of classification

'What's the use of their having names', the Gnat said [referring to insects], 'if they won't answer to them?'

(L. Carroll, *Through the Looking Glass*, ch. 3)

This chapter first discusses the purposes of classification in various disciplines, then looks at the rules which may be applied when classifying, then examines classifications in subjects other than accounting. It is hoped that such study will enable a better analysis of accounting classifications in the following chapters.

2.1 The purposes of classification

As mentioned in Chapter 1, classification is the central activity of librarianship. However, there are many ways in which books could be classified. In a book whose title could be translated[1] as '*To Think, to Classify*', Perec (1985) discusses how books can be classified by, *inter alia*, alphabetical order of author or title, country of author or publication, colour, date of publication or acquisition, language, priority for reading, and so on (p. 39). Not all of these approaches would be useful in a library. Nevertheless, several quite different methods can be found around the world, particularly the Dewey Decimal system and the Library of Congress system. Both of these quite different methods are useful because the main purpose is to store books in a way in which they can be easily found by readers and librarians.

In other fields, classification serves purposes for which some approaches are clearly more useful than others. Classification was one of the earliest activities in the development of organised and scientific study in many disciplines. In the physical sciences it has been a basic tool of understanding. The Mendeleev table of elements (see Figure 2.1) and the Linnaean system are fundamental to chemistry and biology. Such classifications 'sharpen description and analysis' (AAA, 1977, p. 97) and help to reveal underlying structures. This enables prediction of the properties of a chemical element or an animal based on its place in a classification. For example, one could predict the behaviour of iodine from a study of chlorine and bromine and their relationship to iodine in Figure 2.1.

1 H																	2 He
3 Li	4 Be											5 B	6 C	7 N	8 O	9 F	10 Ne
11 Na	12 Mg											13 Al	14 Si	15 P	16 S	17 Cl	18 Ar
19 K	20 Ca	21 Sc	22 Ti	23 V	24 Cr	25 Mn	26 Fe	27 Co	28 Ni	29 Cu	30 Zn	31 Ga	32 Ge	33 As	34 Se	35 Br	36 Kr
37 Rb	38 Sr	39 Y	40 Zr	41 Nb	42 Mo	43 Tc	44 Ru	45 Rh	46 Pd	47 Ag	48 Cd	49 In	50 Sn	51 Sb	52 Te	53 I	54 Xe
55 Ca	56 Ba	57 La	72 Hf	73 Ta	74 W	75 Re	76 Oa	77 Ir	78 Pt	79 Au	80 Hg	81 Tl	82 Pb	83 Bi	84 Po	85 At	86 Rn
87 Fr	88 Ra	89 Ac	104 Rf	105 Ha													

58 Ce	59 Pr	60 Nd	61 Pm	62 Sm	63 Eu	64 Gd	65 Tb	66 Dy	67 Ho	68 Er	69 Tm	70 Yb	71 Lu
90 Th	91 Pa	92 U	93 Np	94 Pu	95 Am	96 Cm	97 Bk	98 Cf	99 Es	100 Pm	101 Md	102 No	103 Lr

Key: For example | 17 Cl | means { atomic number (e.g. number of protons) = 17 / name of element = Chlorine

Figure 2.1 Periodic table of elements.

Further, in the physical sciences, classification has provided insights into what elements or animals once existed, might exist in the future or do exist and wait to be discovered. Chemists in the late nineteenth and early twentieth centuries searched for and found various elements predicted by the table of elements (Aldersley-Williams, 2011).

The Mendeleev classification is uncontroversial, much neater and more stable than the biological classification. But taxonomy in biology retains its interest and central importance. It is this very lack of certainty which makes it of interest for scientists, too. From time to time, new animals are discovered or new theories propounded which cause revisions to the biological classification. As it can tell us much about classification problems in a complex area, the biological system will be examined in some detail later. Figure 2.2 illustrates the detail to which the classification system can go by showing the full zoological hierarchy of the timber wolf of the Canadian subarctic.

2.2 Types of classification

There are several ways of classifying. The simplest forms might be 'dichotomous grouping' (e.g. black things versus non-black things) or 'rank ordering' (e.g. by height of students in a class). More complex classifications include 'dimensioning' (e.g. the periodic table of elements) and 'systematising' (e.g. the Linnaean biological system). Figure 2.2 shows a large and apparently ordered classification system. However, the number of ranks in the biological classification is not constant throughout, and the characteristics for classification do not

Kingdom: Animalia
  Subkingdom: Metazoa
    Phylum: Chordata
      Subphylum: Vertebrata
        Superclass: Tetrapoda
          Class: Mammalia
            Subclass: Theria
              Infraclass: Eutheria
                Cohort: Ferungulata
                  Superorder: Ferae
                    Order: Carnivora
                      Suborder: Fissipeda
                        Superfamily: Canoidea
                          Family: Canidae
                            Subfamily: Caninae
                              Tribe: none for this group
                                Genus: Canis
                                  Subgenus: none for this group
                                    Species: Canis Lupus
                                      Subspecies: Canis Lupus Occidentalis

Figure 2.2 Zoological hierarchy of the timber wolf.

Note
Italicised taxa are obligatory, see Table 2.1.

stay the same throughout. One rule is that certain ranks in the hierarchy are obligatory. This is illustrated for man in Table 2.1.

Two ways of arriving at more complex classifications are 'multidimensional scaling' (MDS) and 'morphological structuring'. MDS uses two or more characteristics on different axes to try to find clusters of elements displaying similar characteristics. It will be used in Chapter 6. Morphological structuring seeks to compose a 'morphology' which lists elements by differentiating factors; it should then be clearer which elements are similar to each other (see the discussion of political systems below).

Table 2.1 Obligatory hierarchy of ranks (example of man)

Kingdom:	Animalia
Phylum:	Chordata
Class:	Mammalia
Order:	Primates
Family:	Hominidae
Genus:	Homo
Species:	Homo sapiens

2.3 Some more examples of classification

Outside the 'hard' sciences, there have also been many classifications. The purposes of classification in the international comparative study in the social sciences are analogous to some of those in the physical sciences. At the most basic level, there may be use, for example, in being able to define 'mixed economies' or 'centrally controlled economies' and then to refer to particular countries as falling into one classification or another. In the social sciences, classifiers suffer from problems similar to those in any other area of social science work. That is, compared to the physical sciences, there is vagueness, uncertainty and a lack of progress in formulating generally agreed theories even on the most fundamental of matters. Some examples of such classifications follow.

Languages

Classification of languages is a fascinating field, bearing some resemblances to biology. It gradually came to be recognised that there was a family of Indo-European languages during the eighteenth century, particularly after the study of Sanskrit. The idea that all these languages came from a common prehistoric source seems first to have been stated in 1786 by a Sanskrit scholar, Sir William Jones. Classification within that family proceeded throughout the nineteenth century, starting with a treatise on inflexional endings in Sanskrit, Greek, Latin, Persian and Germanic in 1816 by Franz Bopp. Table 2.2 shows similarities in basic words for some of the languages in the Indo-European family. Appendix I shows a broad classification of many of the world's existing languages.

As in biology, classification is in effect performed on a genetic or heredity basis. In the case of the Romance languages the 'fossil record' is extremely clear in the preservation of Latin and vulgar forms of it down through the centuries. In the case of Germanic languages, the record is not so clear, so a 'primitive Germanic' language is postulated and study is made instead of common inflexions, pronunciations, basic vocabulary and so on (Bloomfield 1935).

A fascinating link between classification of languages and accounting is found in a paper by Jeanjean *et al.* (2010). The authors use a country's language

Table 2.2 Indo-European languages

English	mother	two	three	is
Sanskrit	mātā	dvau	trayah	asti
Greek	mētēr	duo	treis	esti
Latin	m̄ater	duo	trēs	est
French	mère	deux	trois	est
Italian	madre	due	tre	e
German	Mutter	zwei	drei	ist
Russian	mat'	dva	tri	jest'

Note
Dutch, Danish, Swedish, Polish, Serbian and Spanish all fit in with this table. Even less closely related languages like Persian, Welsh and Armenian fit well.

as an independent variable for explaining whether its companies choose to have their annual reports translated into English. The hypothesis is that greater distance from English will increase cost and difficulty, creating a barrier. The authors present a table, shown here (in extract) as Table 2.3. Readers are encouraged to look carefully at Table 2.3 to judge whether it fits with common sense and with Table 2.2 and Appendix 1. For example, look at the scores of Mandarin Chinese, French and Turkish. Is Mandarin really the same distance from English as French is? Is Turkish really closer to English than Spanish is? On tracking the data through to its source (Dow and Karunaratna, 2006), we discover a simple typographical error which led to a heading in the wrong place, which caused English and German to be recorded as Altaic (e.g. Turkish) languages rather than as Indo-European.

Political systems

Political systems were grouped by Aristotle into three forms of government, using as a first factor the number and wealth of those who held formal authority in the state. He then subdivided these categories according to whether those who held authority were concerned with community or private well-being. Thus he arrived at monarchy-tyranny, aristocracy-oligarchy, *politeia*-democracy. He further subdivided: for example, monarchy is split into five types.

A great deal more recently, political systems have been grouped into political democracies, tutelary democracies, modernising oligarchies, totalitarian oligarchies and traditional oligarchies (Shils 1966). More attempts have been made, like Aristotle's, to use morphologies to help with political classification, as Table 2.4 shows. This can be carried considerably further as shown in Figure 2.3,

Table 2.3 Erroneous scores on 'language distance'

Language	Language distance from English
Danish	3
Dutch	2
Finnish	5
French	5
German	2
Greek	4
Hebrew	5
Indonesian	5
Italian	5
Japanese	5
Mandarin	5
Norwegian	3
Portuguese	5
Spanish	5
Swedish	3
Turkish	4

Source: prepared by the author from Jeanjean *et al.* (2010).

Table 2.4 A political morphology on two factors

	Coercion (fear)	Manipulation (deference)	Regimentation (sentiments)	Persuasional bargaining (cognition/interests)
Participation	Indonesia	Afghanistan Iran	Mexico Tanzania	USA UK France
Exclusion	Iraq Burma Argentina	Saudi Arabia	Albania USSR	

Source: Finer (1970, p. 45).

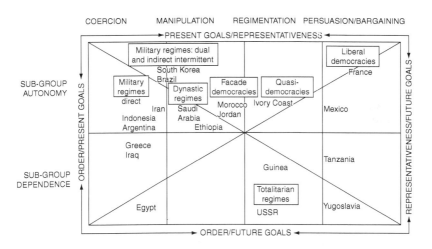

Figure 2.3 A political clustering (source: as Table 2.4).

which could be used for clustering. Such classification activity is abundant in comparative politics; another example is shown in Figure 2.4.

Economies

Economic systems have been divided into capitalism, socialism, communism and fascism; or into traditional economies, market economies and planned economies. Somewhat greater detail has also been attempted (see Table 2.5).

One pair of classifiers of economic systems identified four fundamental differentiating factors and constructed a type of morphology based on this (Gregory and Stuart, 1980, p. 21). The four factors are decision-making structure, mechanisms for information and co-ordination, property rights and incentives. The morphology is shown in Table 2.6 and implies a three-group classification. It has been up-dated in Gregory and Stuart (2003).

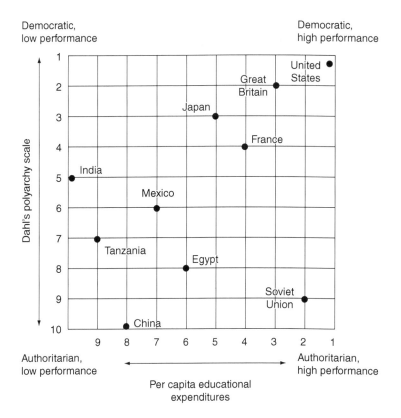

Figure 2.4 Selected nations ranked by political competitiveness and performance (source: Almond, 1966, p. 28).

Note
The indicator of performance is per capita governmental expenditure on education.

Legal systems

Legal systems have also been classified (Kagan, 1955). David and Brierley (1978) produced a four-group classification: Romano-Germanic, Common Law, Socialist and Philosophical-Religious. Table 2.7 shows a classification of some countries into the two legal systems which dominate developed Western countries: common law and Romano-Germanic (code) law.

David and Brierley (1978, p. 20) mention two criteria for determining whether two systems are in the same group. Systems are said to be in the same group if 'someone educated in ... one law will then be capable, without much difficulty, of handling [the other]'. This is somewhat vague and more useful for such a four-group classification than for a more detailed one. However, it might be regarded as a necessary condition for two systems to be of the same 'species'. For example, on this basis, the English spoken in the UK and the USA may be

Table 2.5 Economic systems classification

Family	Species	
Tradition		Traditional
Market	Decentralised	Perfectly competitive market Imperfectly competitive market
	Centralised	Oscar Lange model I Central market survey
Planned market		Indicative planning Visible hand
Plan	Decentralised	Oscar Lange model II
	Centralised	Oscar Lange model III Centralized command Centralized solidarity

Source: Neuberger and Duffy (1976, p. 103).

Table 2.6 Economic systems morphology

	Capitalism	*Market socialism*	*Planned socialism*
Decision-making structure	Primarily decentralized	Primarily decentralized	Primarily centralized
Mechanisms for information	Primarily market	Primarily market	Primarily plan
Property rights	Primarily private ownership	Primarily collective ownership	Primarily state ownership
Incentives	Primarily material	Material and moral	Material and moral

Source: Gregory and Stewart (1980).

Table 2.7 Examples of countries in two legal systems

Common law	Codified Roman law
England and Wales	France
Ireland	Italy
United States	Germany
Canada	Spain
Australia	Netherlands
New Zealand	Japan (commercial)

Note
The laws of Scotland, Israel, South Africa, Quebec, Louisiana and the Philippines embody elements of both systems.

said to be of the same 'species'. The definition may also suggest that the accounting practices of those countries are also within the same 'species'.

The second criterion is that the two systems must not be 'founded on opposed philosophical, political or economic principles'. This would ensure that systems in the same group not only have similar superficial characteristics, but also have similar fundamental structures and influences on development, and are likely to react to new circumstances in similar ways.

Conclusion on 'soft' disciplines

All the social science classifications have been rudimentary, involving no more than splitting systems into a few groups, which are perhaps not precisely defined or exhaustive. Also the methods of classification have been subjective and based on personal knowledge and descriptive literature. These 'shortcomings' are difficult to avoid because of the complexity and 'greyness' in social sciences. However, judgement is inevitable in classification, as will be explained in the next two sections of this chapter.

2.3 Goldilocks and the forebears

This section examines the degree to which classification is determined by who is classifying. Bloor (1982, p. 268) found new support for the claim of Durkheim and Mauss (1903) that the classification of things reproduces a pattern of social arrangements more than a pattern of the things. He argued that even such renowned scientists as Newton and Boyle were affected by their religious and political ideals and 'were arranging the fundamental laws and classifications of their natural knowledge in a way that artfully aligned them with their social goals' (p. 290). The fields of cosmology and anthropology are used as examples below.

Cosmology

Throughout most of recorded history, man[2] saw himself as the unique peak of creation (see below). He lived in a world which was also in a class of its own, being fixed and at the centre of the universe. The Copernican revolution, set in motion in 1543 by the publication of the book commonly known as the '*Revolutions*',[3] spread slowly. For espousing it, Galileo was held under house arrest from 1633 to his death in 1642. Even in unorthodox Amsterdam, Joan Blaeu's *New and Very Accurate Map of the Whole World* of 1662 still gave equal status to Ptolemy's geocentric beliefs and heliocentrism (Brotton, 2012, p. 288). However, enlightenment eventually reduced anthropocentrism: the earth is now classified as a planet (i.e. something that moves) orbiting a star which is rather far from the middle of one of many galaxies. The planet is fairly small, but happens to be in the Goldilocks zone: at the right distance from its star to be at a congenial temperature for water-based life forms.

Anthropology

The 'great chain of being', derived from Aristotle and conventional for millennia, is a six-group classification[4] (Lovejoy, 1964). Man is not classified as an animal at all but as a special creation which is a little lower than the angels. They had spirit only, animals had body only, but man had both. Man saw himself as unique: not just *sui generis* but *hors de catégorie*. In the eighteenth century, Linnaeus took *homo sapiens* down a rung by placing him in the animal kingdom, though he remained *sui generis*. The descent of man continued in the nineteenth century when Darwin outrageously suggested evolution from more 'primitive' primates, presumably without spirits; and other types of humans joined his genus, such as *homo neanderthalensis*. In the twentieth century, the genus got more crowded, for example with the arrival of *homo floresiensis*. In the twenty-first century, Wildman *et al.* (2003) went yet further by proposing[5] that, since modern humans share 99.4 per cent of non-synonymous DNA with chimpanzees, *homo sapiens* is a parvenu member of their genus.

2.4 Classification and standards

The previous section showed how classification can depend on the mindsets of those doing the classifying, and how classification can therefore change dramatically over time without the objects changing. This section examines the degree to which classification depends upon the characteristics chosen to measure the objects being classified, and on the definition of the characteristics. Foucault (1970, p. 125) suggested that modernity in science begins with privileging observation, starting with Roger Bacon. Sight must replace reliance on 'self-evident' axioms. It also replaces hearsay evidence about sightings, and it is given greater weight than the less reliable senses of taste, smell and touch (p. 132). The invention of the telescope and the microscope helped greatly. It is observation which guided Copernicus and Galileo, and Linnaeus and Darwin. However, not even everything visible is relevant and reliable: colour is not (p. 133). When Linnaeus classified plants, he used only four observable features: the shape of elements, the quantity of the elements, their arrangement related to each other and their relative magnitudes. However, there was still much scope in deciding which elements to observe, as will be explained below. The fields of cosmology, chemistry, biology and medicine are now used as examples.

Cosmology

Whether or not a celestial body is classed as a planet depends, like any classification, on standards.[6] The 'standard' for a planet was revised by the International Astronomical Union in 2006 (IAU, 2006), with the result that Pluto (which had only become a planet, as far as we were concerned, on its discovery in 1930) ceased to be one. The revision was caused by the discovery of bodies larger than Pluto with orbits further from the sun. The re-definition of a planet and the re-classification of Pluto has both scientific and cultural implications (Basri and Brown, 2006), though not as large as those that led to the arrest of Galileo for professing the planetary status of the earth. An important implication for other classifications (e.g. in accounting) is that an object's place in a classification can depend on the range of objects being classified.

Chemistry

Some alchemists had classified elements into solids, liquids and gases, but this is now seen to produce an unhelpful classification of such liquids as mercury, molten lead and liquid nitrogen. So, chemists moved on to observing various behaviours of elements (e.g. reaction to oxygen), leading to Mendeleev's periodic table (Aldersley-Williams, 2011). This approach was later confirmed by a more fundamental one when it became possible to count protons, neutrons and electrons.

Biology

Linnaeus started his classifying with plants, perhaps because their characteristics are more easily observable than such things as the structure of the inner ear of animals (Foucault, 1970, p. 137). However, he chose to ignore differences in leaves, stems and roots, such that the 'primary arrangement of the vegetables[7] is to be taken from the fruit-body[8] alone' (Linnaeus, 1751, s. 164). In other words, his system was essentially arbitrary. Whereas the features of living plants are easy to observe, plants lack a fossil record on which to base the evolutionary approach that was adopted fairly early on for animal classification. However, analysis of plant DNA has recently solved this problem and led to a transformation of the botanical classification to something 'natural', i.e. related to the thing causing the variation (e.g. Duff and Nickrent, 1999).

Classification of animals has a long history. Socrates classified man as a 'featherless biped', but his pupil Plato was mocked by Diogenes for repeating it. Ironically, biologists still include humans and birds in a super-class of tetrapoda. However, at a more detailed level, humans are not now classed with birds but with dogs and dolphins (which ostensibly have four feet and no feet, respectively). Looking more deeply, one can observe five fingers not only on a human hand but also on a dog's front paw and inside a dolphin's flipper. Several other mammalian shared characteristics can be identified, such as giving birth to live young.

As with plants, Linnaeus classified animals by observing shared characteristics, but the result again depends upon which characteristics are chosen. As a result, many of Linnaeus' animal classifications have also been overturned. Classification now rests on a search for homologues, which are shared characteristics inherited from a common ancestor, such as seen in the hand, paw and flipper. In effect, zoological classification is now entirely about descent. For this purpose, the analysis of DNA became a powerful tool as a supplement to, and sometimes as a contradiction of, the received fossil record (Stringer, 2011, ch. 1). Again, the zoological classification is now regarded as 'natural' (i.e. less arbitrary, being based on evolutionary relationships as evidenced by DNA).

However, a caveat should be entered. The biologists' classifications take no account of different possible purposes. For example, if the purpose were to help in planning the habitats or menus for a new zoological park, it might be more useful to classify a dolphin with a shark even though the dolphin is much more closely related to a dog, a human or even a pterodactyl.[9]

Diseases

Medicine is a practical activity, which relies heavily on the International Classification of Diseases (ICD). This has been in operation for a century but is revised approximately every decade (Bowker and Star, 2000, p. 136). The ICD is a pragmatic tool with a clear purpose: it helps doctors to identify diseases and then to record information about patients. Whereas biologists now classify in a monothetic way, using binary characteristics (e.g. backbone or not), the ICD looks for a number of shared characteristics (a polythetic system). Further, whereas chemical elements do not change,[10] and animal species change very slowly, diseases change rapidly. Lastly, the ICD sometimes needs to be dramatically expanded. It began among six European countries, but had to be adjusted when African and Asian diseases were included (Bowker and Star, 2000, p. 151). Many of these features remind one of classifications of accounting systems: they are polythetic, the systems change rapidly and the classifications started with Europe and North America only.

What's in a name?

A more alarming point must also be made: no classifications are 'real'. As Buffon pointed out in 1749:

> The more we increase the number of divisions in the production of nature, the closer we shall approach to the true, since nothing really exists in nature except individuals, and since genera, orders and classes exist only in our imagination.
>
> (as cited in Foucault, 1970, p. 146)

We noted earlier that the definition of a planet is a matter of opinion. In biology, it is notable that neither Darwin nor any follower has set out a definition of 'species' which has gained general acceptance. Linnaeus thought that species were fixed in number, immutable in nature and divinely created. Darwin showed that the first two points were errors, and drew a polite veil over the third. However, we can now put another interpretation on the origin of species: they evolved in the brain of *homo sapiens*. The lack of definitions explains why there is debate about whether Neanderthals and modern humans are part of the same species (given that they have successfully interbred),[11] and whether humans are part of the chimpanzee genus. Buffon's insight has not yet been taken to its logical conclusion, but the complete abandonment of the apparatus of species, genera, etc. has been contemplated by biologists (Mishler, 2009, p. 65).

The fact that no classifications are real does not mean that classification cannot be useful. As noted earlier, for librarians or medics, various competing classification systems could be almost as useful as each other. Linnaeus' initial botanical classification was also of practical use in organising information, even though it was arbitrary. However, Mendeleev's classification in chemistry was much more useful than some earlier classifications because it identified 'missing' elements and predicted what they would be like.

Accounting classifiers can learn from these fields. One relevant lesson from above is the need for detailed personal observation. Another is that the purposes of a classification should be considered. Further, classifiers should be deliberate about the characteristics measured; Roberts (1995, p. 641) shows 'the incoherence of taxonomies which rely upon appeals to objectivity'. We apply these lessons later in the book, when analysing past accounting classifications.

Notes

1 A translation of *Penser/Classer* was published in 2009 by Godine Press of Boston under the less literal title of *Thoughts of Sorts*.
2 We use the term 'man' when discussing authors who did so (i.e. those until the late twentieth century).
3 *De revolutionibus orbium coelestium* (On the revolutions of the heavenly spheres).
4 God, angels, man, animals, plants and minerals.
5 This proposal has not been generally accepted. For example, Steiper and Young (2006, p. 385) still treat *homo* and *pan* as different genera.
6 At first sight, the word 'standard' has a different meaning in financial reporting from that used here. It appears to refer to a type of regulation. Elsewhere in accounting, a 'standard cost' fits more obviously into the normal scientific meaning. However, the documents issued by the International Accounting Standards Board (IASB), for example, are not in themselves requirements. The IASB is a private sector standard setter. A regulator such as the European Union can choose to require certain companies to comply with a standard.
7 That is, plants; Linnaeus classified all things on earth as animal, vegetable or mineral.
8 That is, the reproductive system.
9 The four types of animal in this sentence other than the shark are all in the tetrapod clade.
10 Elements cannot be changed by chemical reactions. They can be changed by (and indeed were formed by) nuclear reactions. Thus, gold is created from other elements such as base metals (ultimately from hydrogen) and it could be used to create even heavier elements, but this does not change the nature, definition or 'standard' of gold.
11 Modern humans, except for sub-Saharan Africans, contain traces of Neanderthal DNA; up to 4 per cent in some cases (Green *et al.*, 2010).

3 International differences in accounting

3.1 Introduction

This book is about international classification of accounting systems, but the topic is only interesting if there are important international differences in accounting. Dozens of books and hundreds of academic papers deal with that field. Some of its themes are summarised in this chapter, especially where they are connected to classification.

The chapter begins by looking at how different cultures, laws and financing systems might have caused different accounting. Since the cultures, laws and financing systems can be classified, the classifications in those domains might predict a classification of accounting systems. These factors that lie behind accounting have not been affected by the arrival of IFRS. Therefore, they might cause different countries to respond to IFRS differently. The chapter also examines that issue.

3.2 Reasons for accounting differences

Many reasons have been suggested in the literature for international differences in financial reporting. Some authors state that they are merely listing plausible reasons; few provide precise hypotheses or tests of them, as noted by Meek and Saudagaran (1990). Wallace and Gernon (1991) complained about the lack of theory in international comparative accounting.

The literature (e.g. Choi and Mueller, 1992, ch. 2; Radebaugh and Gray, 1993, ch. 3; Belkaoui, 1995, ch. 2; Nobes and Parker, 2012, ch. 1) offers a large number of possible reasons for international differences (see Table 3.1). Schweikart (1985) and Harrison and McKinnon (1986) provide some elements of a general theory, without specifying which factors are major explanatory variables for accounting practices.

Two somewhat similar theoretical models of the reasons for accounting differences are those of Gray (1988) and of Doupnik and Salter (1995). Gray suggests a model based on cultural factors, as examined later. Doupnik and Salter provide a synthesis of previous discussions leading to a framework, which is simplified here as in Figure 3.1 so that an alternative can be proposed later. One

Table 3.1 Reasons previously proposed for international accounting differences

1 Nature of business ownership and financing system
2 Colonial inheritance
3 Invasions
4 Taxation
5 Inflation
6 Level of education
7 Age and size of accountancy profession
8 Stage of economic development
9 Legal systems
10 Culture
11 History
12 Geography
13 Language
14 Influence of theory
15 Political systems, social climate
16 Religion
17 Accidents

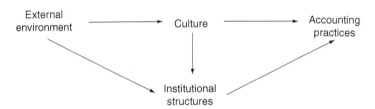

Figure 3.1 A simplification of DS's model of development (source: adapted from Doupnik and Salter, 1995, exhibit 1).

difficulty emerging from Figure 3.1 is that four of the ten variables (see Table 3.2) are cultural (based on Gray) and six are institutional, but culture is seen as giving rise to the institutions. This suggests the possibility of double counting. A related difficulty with Doupnik and Salter is that there is no attempt to connect their six institutional factors to see whether they might cause each other. In particular, four of the six (taxation, inflation, level of education and stage of economic development) may not be necessary, as suggested below.

3.3 Some terminological issues

A number of terminological issues are raised by studying the above literature. These need to be addressed before attempting to develop a general model. One of the problems of identifying reasons for differences, and perhaps then classifying accounting systems, is a lack of clarity about what is being examined or classified. This book frequently discusses accounting *practices*, using 'accounting' to mean published financial reporting. In some jurisdictions, the *rules* of financial reporting may be identical, or very similar, to the practices, but sometimes a

Table 3.2 DS's independent variables

Cultural	Institutional
Individualism	Legal system
Power distance	Capital market
Uncertainty avoidance	Tax
Masculinity	Inflation levels
	Level of education
	Level of economic development

Source: Doupnik and Salter (1995).

company may depart from rules or may have to make choices in the absence of rules. The Price Waterhouse data, used by many researchers (see Chapter 4), seem to contain a mix of *de facto* and *de jure* aspects 'in a perplexing way' (Rahman *et al.*, 1996).

Another difficulty concerns the word 'system'. Doupnik and Salter (1995) and Alexander and Archer (2000) use it to cover such things as regulatory agencies. Others (e.g. Nair and Frank, 1980) have concentrated on a corpus of accounting rules or practices. This book follows the latter route, that is, an 'accounting system' is a set of practices used in a published annual report. Although this is a narrow definition, these practices will reflect the wider context in which they operate.

A related point is that most researchers look at classifications of *countries* by their accounting environments or systems. Roberts (1995) highlighted this problem, noting that a country could have more than one system; for example, one system for listed companies and another for small private companies. Similarly, some large listed companies may adopt very different practices from what is 'normal' for most large companies in the country. This became especially obvious in continental Europe, with the use of US rules or international accounting standards by some very large companies from 1993 onwards. It is now common (e.g. in most EU countries) for listed companies to use IFRS for consolidated statements even though national accounting rules are used for other purposes. Since there can be more than one system in a country, it is more useful to specify accounting systems, and then to note that particular companies in particular countries at particular dates are using them. Of course, for labelling purposes, it might be useful to refer, for example, to the system used in 2015 by US public companies.

Also, a country's accounting system may change dramatically over time; for example, as a result of economic or political revolutions (cf. China, Russia, Poland, etc.). Less dramatically, accounting in a country can change quite significantly as a result of new laws (e.g. Spain from the late 1980s as a consequence of EC Directives).[1]

Lastly, companies in two countries (e.g. the UK and Ireland) can use extremely similar accounting practices (i.e. perhaps the same 'system'). In a similar manner to the characteristics of human individuals, the detailed elements of a company's accounting practices can differ so much that the number of different sets of practices is effectively infinite. Nevertheless, it is useful for some purposes to recognise that humans all belong to the same species. The individual members of the species are all different but have certain features in common. By analogy, a certain degree of variation among company practices may be allowed without having to abandon the idea that the companies are all using the same system.

3.4 An initial statement of a general model

Financing systems

The proposal here, which will be explained more fully later, is that the major reason for international differences in financial reporting is different purposes for that reporting. In particular, at a country level, it is suggested that the financing system is relevant in determining the purpose of financial reporting. Zysman (1983) classified financing systems into three types: (a) *capital market based*, in which prices are established in competitive markets, (b) *credit-based system: governmental*, in which resources are administered by the government and (c) *credit-based system: financial institutions*, in which banks and other financial institutions are dominant.

Zysman suggested that the UK and the USA have a type (a) system, France and Japan a type (b) system and Germany a type (c) system. According to Zysman, in all systems companies rely considerably on their own profits for capital but their external sources of funds differ. Where external long-term finance is important, securities are the main source in the capital market system. In such countries, there is a wide range of capital instruments and of financial institutions, and the latter have an arm's length relationship with companies. Investors change their holdings through the secondary securities markets, which are large. In credit-based systems, the capital market is smaller, so companies are more reliant on whoever grants credit. This usually means banks, whether under the influence of governments or not. Cable (1985) examined the importance of banks in the German economic system. In this system, investors will find it more difficult to adjust their holdings, so they may be more interested in long-run control of the management.

A development of the Zysman classification is proposed, as in Table 3.3. For this, the concept of 'insider' and 'outsider' financiers needs to be developed.

Table 3.3 Financing systems

	Strong credit	Strong equity
Insiders dominant	I	III
Outsiders dominant	II	IV

Source: prepared by the author from Zysman (1983).

This idea of insiders and outsiders, which has its roots in the finance literature, has been used before for accounting purposes (e.g. see Nobes, 1988, p. 31) and to discuss contrasting corporate governance systems (e.g. Franks and Mayer, 1992). 'Outsiders' are not members of the board of directors and do not have a privileged relationship with the company (e.g. such as that enjoyed by a company's banker who is also a major shareholder). They include both private individual shareholders and some institutions. For example, insurance companies and unit trusts normally have widely diversified portfolios, so that any particular holding does not constitute a large proportion of a company's capital. Therefore, such institutions should perhaps be counted as outsiders. By contrast, 'insiders' such as governments, banks, families and other companies are all likely to have close, long-term relationships with their investees. This will involve the private provision of timely and frequent accounting information.

Both of Zysman's credit-based systems fall into category I of Table 3.3. Category II (a credit-based system with a large amount of listed debt with outsider owners) is plausible but uncommon. A possible example is discussed near the end of this subsection. Category III is an equity-based system where most shares are owned by insiders. In Japan, for example, there are large numbers of listed companies and a large equity market capitalisation, but the shares are extensively owned by banks and other companies (Nobes and Parker, 2012, chs 1 and 11).

Category IV systems involve important equity markets with large numbers of outsider shareholders. In these systems there will be a demand for public disclosure and for external audit because more providers of finance have no involvement in management and no private access to financial information. This is the classic setting of most of the finance literature (e.g. Jensen and Meckling, 1976; Beaver, 1989). More recently, a connection between more disclosure and lower cost of equity capital has been examined in such a context (Botosan, 1997). Pursuing this line, I suggest that the key issue for financial reporting is the existence or otherwise of such Category IV financing. Ways of measuring this are noted below.

In a particular country, there may be elements of several of these four systems. For example, small companies are unlikely to be financed by a Category IV system in any country. However, for the moment, let us assume that the economic activity in any country is dominated by one particular financing system. The hypothesis predicting a correlation between the style of corporate financing and the type of accounting system is that the rule-makers for, and the preparers of, financial reports in equity-outsider (Category IV) countries are largely concerned with the outside users. The conceptual frameworks used by the rule-makers of the US, the UK, Australia and the International Accounting Standards Board (IASB) make it clear that this is so. In particular, they state that they are concerned with reporting financial performance and enabling the prediction of future cash flows for relatively sophisticated outsider users of financial statements of large companies. By contrast, credit-based countries (mostly Category I) will be more concerned with the protection of creditors and therefore with the prudent calculation of distributable profit. Their financiers (insiders) will not need externally audited, published reports. This difference of purpose will lead to differences in accounting practices. The less common categories (II and III) will be discussed later.

Empirical researchers have established measures to distinguish the categories (for example, La Porta *et al.*, 1997). These can include the number of domestic listed companies in a country (or this deflated by size of population), the equity market capitalisation (or this deflated by GDP) and the proportion of shares held by 'outsiders'. Although the boundary between the types of financing system may sometimes be unclear (as in many of the classifications in social science, languages, law or, even, biology), the contrast between a strong equity-outsider system and other systems should be clear enough, as Table 3.4 demonstrates for some countries.

It is proposed that financial reporting systems should be divided initially into two classes, for the moment labelled as A and B. Class A corresponds to what some have called Anglo-Saxon accounting and Class B to continental European. To assist researchers in measuring a system, some core features of the two systems are suggested in Table 3.5. For example, systems of Class A will share all, or a large proportion of, the practices shown for that class.

It is proposed that, for developed countries,[2] the extent to which a particular country is associated with Class A or Class B accounting is predictable on the basis of its position with respect to financing systems. If the present accounting system was developed in the past, then reference to the past importance of financing systems will be relevant. Strong equity-outsider markets (Category IV) lead to Class A systems; otherwise Class B systems prevail.

However, even if a particular country is traditionally associated with weak equity markets and therefore Class B accounting, the country might change. For example, China changed in the direction of a strong equity-outsider market and Class A accounting (Chow *et al.*, 1995). However, the accounting might remain stuck in the past for legal or other reasons of inertia. Nevertheless, in some countries, certain companies might be especially commercially affected. They might

Table 3.4 Equity market measures

	Domestic equity market capitalisation/GDP	Domestic listed companies per million of population
UK	1.34	30.2
Netherlands	0.99	14.4
Sweden	0.76	24.4
Belgium	0.50	14.3
France	0.40	12.4
Spain	0.36	9.3
Germany	0.18	8.4
Italy	0.18	4.3

Source: *European Stock Exchange Statistics, Annual Report 1995*, Federation of European Stock Exchanges; and *Pocket World in Figures 1995*, The Economist.

Table 3.5 Examples of features of the two accounting classes

Feature	Class A	Class B
Depreciation and pensions	Accounting practice differs from tax rules	Accounting practice follows tax rules
Measurement of financial assets (equities)	Fair value	Lower of cost and market
Unsettled currency gains	Taken to income	Deferred or not recognised
Legal reserves	Not found	Required
Profit and loss format	Expenses recorded by function (e.g. cost of sales)	Expenses recorded by nature (e.g. total wages)
Cash flow statements	Required	Not required, found only sporadically

adopt Class A accounting by using flexibility in the national rules, by breaking national rules, or by producing two sets of financial statements. Some German examples of these routes can be given. Bayer's consolidated financial statements (for 1994 to 1997) used non-typical German practices, that were different from those used in its parent's statements, in order to comply with International Accounting Standards (IAS). Further, officials of the Ministry of Finance announced that departure from German rules would be 'tolerated' for such group accounts.[3] In the case of Deutsche Bank (e.g. for 1995), two full sets of financial statements were produced, under German rules and IAS, respectively.

This was resolved when a German law of 1998 allowed the use of IAS or US GAAP for the consolidated statements of listed companies. Then, of course, IFRS became compulsory in the EU for this purpose under the EU Regulation of 2002.

A related issue is that, as noted earlier, there are two aspects of financial reporting which can be separated: measurement and disclosure (e.g. Nair and Frank, 1980). As explained below, the measurement issues seem to be driven by the equity/creditor split, and the disclosure issues by the outsider/insider split. The equity/creditor split leads to different kinds of *objectives* for financial reporting. As suggested earlier, systems serving equity markets are required to provide relevant information on performance and the assessment of future cash flows in order to help with the making of financial decisions. Systems in a creditor environment are required to calculate prudent and reliable distributable (and taxable) profit. By contrast, the outsider/insider split leads to different *amounts* of information: where outsiders are important, there is a demand for more published financial reporting.

It has been assumed here that equity financing systems are normally those which are associated with large numbers of outsiders, so that Class A systems are an amalgam of equity and outsider features. However, if there were countries (Category II of Table 3.3) with large markets for listed debt but not for listed equities, then one might expect a financial reporting system with the high disclosures of Class A but the measurement rules of Class B. Perhaps the closest example of a system with Class B measurement rules but high disclosures is the German system for listed companies. Germany does indeed have an unusually large market in listed debt.

This way of distinguishing between the forces acting on measurement and those acting on disclosure may help to resolve the difficulties of a cultural explanation as discussed by Baydoun and Willett (1995, pp. 82–88).

Category III (equity-insider) financing would not produce Class A accounting because published financial reporting is unimportant. The main financiers may be interested in performance and cash flows but they have access to private 'management' information.

Colonial inheritance

Some countries are affected by very strong external cultural influences, perhaps due to their small size or underdeveloped state or former colonial status. Such culturally dominated countries are likely to be using an accounting system based on that of the influential country even if this seems inappropriate to their current commercial needs (Hove, 1986).

Colonial inheritance (Factor 2 in Table 3.1) is probably the major explanatory factor for the general system of financial reporting in many countries outside Europe (Briston, 1978). It is easy to predict how accounting will work in Gambia (British) compared to neighbouring Senegal (French). The same general point applies to Singapore (Briston and Liang, 1990) or Australia (Miller, 1994). Colonial inheritance extends of course to legal systems and to other background and cultural factors, not just to direct imports of accounting (Parker, 1989). Allied to this are the effects of substantial investment from another country, which may lead to accountants and accounting migrating together with the capital.

Another influence is invasions (Factor 3) which may lead to major effects on accounting, as is the case with Japanese,[4] French[5] and German[6] accounting. However, when the invader retires, any foreign accounting can be gradually removed if it does not suit the country: Japan closed down its Securities and Exchange Commission when the Americans left, whereas France retained its accounting plan in order to aid reconstruction after the Second World War (Standish, 1990).

3.5 Why other factors may be less useful

If the above conclusions are accepted (i.e. that a general two-class model of financial reporting systems can be built which rests on only the importance of financing systems and colonial inheritance), then most of the 17 factors listed in Table 3.1 seem unnecessary as explanatory independent variables, at least for the initial two-class classification. This section explains why.

Tax

Previous writers (e.g. Nobes, 1983b) have not been helpful by listing tax as one of the major causes of accounting differences. These writers have, in effect, suggested that Class A accounting systems are not dominated by tax rules whereas Class B systems are; and, therefore, that the tax difference is one of the reasons for the difference in accounting systems. However, the disconnection of tax from accounting in Class A systems may be seen as a *result* of the existence of a competing purpose for accounting rather than the major cause of international accounting differences. Lamb *et al.* (1998) look at this in detail, concluding:

1   Rules for the determination of the taxable profit of businesses will be important in all countries (assuming that taxation of profit is significant).
2   Without some major competing purpose for accounting for which tax rules are unsuitable, tax rules made by governments will therefore tend to dominate accounting, so that tax practices and accounting practices are the same (as in Class B).
3   In some countries (or for some companies), there is the major competing purpose of supplying financial reports to equity-outsider markets (for which tax rules are unsuitable). In this case, for many accounting topics, there will be two sets of accounting rules (and practices): tax rules and financial reporting rules (as in Class A).

Consequently, the tax variable is not needed to explain the difference between Class A and Class B systems. Nevertheless, for those systems where tax and accounting are closely linked (Class B), international differences in tax rules do create international accounting differences. However, these are detailed differences *within* a class of accounting systems which all share the major feature of being dominated by tax rules, which is one of the distinguishing marks of the class.

There is a further important connection here. The equity/credit split in financing, as discussed earlier, coincides with the proposed equity-user/tax-user split: accounting systems designed to serve creditors are systems dominated by tax rules. This is because the calculation of the legally distributable profit (to protect creditors) and the calculation of taxable profit are both issues in which governments are interested. The calculation of legally distributable profit is a different purpose from the calculation of taxable profit but it is not 'competing' in the sense of requiring a different set of rules because both calculations benefit from precision in the rules[7] and from the minimisation of the use of judgement, which is not the case for the estimation of cash flows.

Legal systems

For developed Western countries and for many others (e.g. Japan, South America and most of Africa), it is possible to classify countries neatly into codified legal systems and common law systems (David and Brierley, 1985), as discussed in Section 2.3. This is of great relevance to the regulatory system for accounting. There is a high degree of correlation between equity-outsider financing systems and common law countries, and between credit-insider systems and codified law.[8] On the whole, therefore, the same groupings would result from using a legal system variable rather than from using a financing system variable. This again suggests the possibility of double counting. The exception of the Netherlands, which raises further doubts about using the legal variable for accounting classification, is explained below.

For culturally dominated countries, both the legal and accounting systems are likely to have been imported from the same place, so the correlation between these two variables is unsurprising. Both factors can be explained by the colonial influence factor, so the legal factor is not needed. For other countries, there may be aspects of the common law system which predispose a country towards the creation of strong equity-outsider systems (La Porta *et al.*, 1997), but going that far back in the causal chain is not necessary for the present model. For the present purposes, it may be more useful to specify the legal variable as the regulatory system for accounting rather than the more general legal system. The variable would be measured by locating the source of the most detailed accounting regulations. A 0/1 variable would contrast (i) rules made by professional accountants, company directors, independent bodies, stock exchanges and equity market regulators, and (ii) rules made by tax authorities, government ministries (other than those concerned primarily with listed companies) and legal bureaucrats.

Once more, it could be argued that this version of the legal variable is not independent but is dependent on the financing variable. In strong equity-outsider systems, commercial pressure gives the strongest power over financial reporting to group (i) because, since the financial reporting for the equity/outsiders uses separate rules from tax rules, there is no need for group (ii) to control them. In particular, many of the disclosures (e.g. consolidated financial reports, cash flow statements, segmental reporting, interim reporting) are not relevant for tax or distribution purposes in most jurisdictions. Financial institutions and large companies are sufficiently powerful to persuade group (ii) to allow financial reporting to respond to commercial needs. In common law countries, the importance of group (i) creates no problems of jurisprudence because non-governmental regulation is commonplace. In the rare case of a codified law country with a strong equity market (e.g. the Netherlands), the regulatory system for financial reporting can still give prominence to group (i) although this creates tensions (Zeff *et al.*, 1992). In all systems, group (ii) retains full control over tax rules.

Level of education

Doupnik and Salter's variable here (see Table 3.2) is the percentage of population with tertiary education. It is hard to see how one could explain the major accounting differences on this basis. Can one explain the large accounting differences between, on the one hand, the UK, the US and the Netherlands (where

Class A dominates) and, on the other hand, France, Germany and Italy (where Class B dominates) on the basis of the rather similar levels of tertiary education? Again, can one explain the remarkable similarities between accounting in Malawi, Nigeria and Zimbabwe (Class A countries) and the UK (also Class A) on the basis of the rather different levels of tertiary education? Instead there seems to be a connection with the 'colonial inheritance' point, as discussed earlier and as taken up again in the 'level of economic development' point below. Thus it is not surprising that the education variable did not help Doupnik and Salter. Previous suggestions related to this factor (e.g. Radebaugh, 1975) seem, more plausibly, to involve the comparison of developed with less developed countries.

Different levels of professional accounting education might be relevant (Shoenthal, 1989), perhaps especially in developing countries (e.g. Parry and Grove, 1990). However, Nobes (1992) casts doubt upon the relevance of this type of factor for classification. To the extent that this is not another issue related to developed versus developing countries, differences in professional education might be covered by Factor 8 in Table 3.1 (age and size of accountancy profession) and may be a *result* of accounting differences rather than their cause.

Level of economic development

It is proposed here that the key issue is not the influence of the stage of economic development on financial reporting (as suggested by Doupnik and Salter). Gernon and Wallace (1995, p. 64) agree that there is 'no conclusive evidence' about the relationship. The problem is that, while many African countries with a low level of development have accounting systems rather like the UK's, some have completely different accounting systems rather like that in France. By contrast, the UK or the Netherlands have a rather similar level of economic development to that of Germany or Italy but completely different accounting systems.

It would seem plausible to argue that, if accounting systems were indigenously created in all countries, then they would develop differently in developed and un-developed economies. However, it is suggested that this point is largely overridden by the proposition that developing countries are likely to be using an accounting system invented elsewhere. Perhaps the system has been forced on them, or they have borrowed it. Either way, it is usually possible to predict accounting in such countries by looking at the source of the external influences. Therefore, the level of development is not the key predictor for the split between Class A and Class B. Cooke and Wallace (1990) seem to support the distinction between developed and developing countries when it comes to the influence of various environmental factors on accounting.

Inflation levels

Another factor included by Doupnik and Salter is the rate of inflation and, once more, previous writers have not been helpful here. For example, although Nobes

(1983) did not include inflation as a key variable, Nobes and Parker (1995, p. 19) suggested that 'Without reference to this factor, it would not be possible to explain accounting differences in countries severely affected by it.' However, on reflection, the more important issue is illustrated by other points that they make in the same section:

1   'accountants in the English-speaking world have proved remarkably immune to inflation when it comes to taking decisive action';
2   'in several South American countries, the most obvious feature ... is the use of methods of general price-level adjustment';
3   'the fact that it was *governments* which responded to inflation in France, Spain, Italy and Greece ... is symptomatic of the regulation of accounting in these countries'.

In other words, any accounting system would have to respond at some level of inflation sustained for a certain length of time.[9] The key points are who responds and how they respond. The nature of these responses to inflation is a good indicator of the regulatory system for accounting. In countries where Class A accounting is dominant, professional accountants respond; in countries where Class B accounting is dominant, governments respond within the framework of the tax system.[10] Differential inflation does not cause the difference between Class A and Class B accounting, the regulators typical to the two classes respond differently to it. However, as with some other factors, differential inflation response may lead to differences between the systems *within* Class A or *within* Class B.

Culture

Culture (defined by Hofstede as 'the collective programming of the mind') is clearly a plausible cause of accounting differences as proposed by Gray's (1988) application of Hofstede's (1980) theory. Doupnik and Salter's four culture variables (see Table 3.2) were drawn from Hofstede. However, the attempt to use cultural variables entails large problems (Gernon and Wallace, 1995, pp. 85, 90, 91). Baydoun and Willett (1995, p. 69) also suggest that the mechanisms of the effects are not obvious, and: 'such is the nature of the concepts involved and the state of the available evidence that it is questionable whether Gray's adaptation of Hofstede's theory can in fact be empirically validated in the usual scientific sense' (p. 72).

   One can agree with Gray that culture can at least be seen as one of the background factors leading to more direct causes of accounting differences (such as the financing system). Culture may be of more direct help when examining other issues, such as differences in the behaviour of auditors (Soeters and Schreuder, 1988). It will also be useful later to divide countries into culturally self-sufficient and culturally dominated. As noted in the previous section, the latter countries (e.g. colonies or former colonies) might be expected to adopt practices from other countries. In this sense, culture might indeed overwhelm other factors for certain countries.

Broad factors

Others of the 17 factors of Table 3.1 are too wide to be useful and can be accommodated within more specific factors. On these grounds, history and geography (Factors 11 and 12) can be removed. In a sense, 'history' explains everything, but this is not helpful unless it is known which part of history. For example, colonial history and the history of the corporate financing system are likely to be particularly relevant, so other factors can cover this.

'Geography' is also too broad a factor to be useful. It seems unlikely that the physical nature of a country has a major effect on its dominant class of accounting. For example, the Netherlands and Belgium have very different accounting, although they are similar in physical environment. By contrast, the UK and Australia have similar accounting although they are dramatically different in climate, terrain and type of agriculture. A country's location may be relevant for other factors (such as colonial inheritance and invasions) or for certain aspects of its financial history (such as the fact that maritime countries may tend to develop certain types of trading or markets). However, the relevant aspects of geography should be picked up by other factors. In the meantime, one merely notes that location seems to be overwhelmed by other factors in the sense that New Zealand has rather similar accounting to the distant UK; and the Netherlands has very different accounting from its neighbours, Germany and Belgium

Covariation

Other factors may involve covariation rather than causation. For example, the fact that many English-speaking countries have similar accounting practices is probably not caused by their shared language (Factor 13): the language was inherited with the accounting or with other factors which affect accounting. Language similarities may contribute to the strength of cultural dominance, and language differences may slow down the transfer of accounting technology. However, these points do not make language a key independent variable.

Theory

Theory (Factor 14), in the form of an explicit or implicit underlying framework, is certainly of relevance in some countries.[11] However, there are always competing theories (as examined for accounting by Watts and Zimmerman, 1979). It is suggested here that the degree of acceptance of particular accounting theories within a country *depends upon* other factors, such as the strength of equity markets and the regulatory system.

Results rather than causes

Some factors above have been seen to be more results than causes of the major accounting differences. Similarly, the age and size of the accountancy professions (Factor 7) differ substantially around the world,[12] but this is likely to be the *result* of different accounting systems. For example, the comparatively small size of the German auditing profession seems to result from the comparatively small number of audited companies, which in turn results from comparative weakness of equity markets.

Factors more relevant outside the developed world

Certain other factors might not discriminate between developed Western countries, on which most classifications have concentrated. For example, political systems (Factor 15), religion (Factor 16) and stage of economic development (Factor 8) are probably sufficiently homogeneous in these countries that they do not have major explanatory power. They might well be relevant for a broader study, and at levels of classification below the two major classes. For example, religion may have an effect on accounting in some countries (Gambling and Abdel-Karim, 1991; Hamid *et al.*, 1993). Of course, religion and culture may be closely related.

Accidents

Close examination of accidents (Factor 17) will generally reveal their causes. However, certainly at the level of detailed accounting practices within a class, 'accident' may be a useful summary explanation. For example, some of the largest differences between US and UK accounting (LIFO, deferred tax and goodwill) in the 1990s could be said to be accidental causes.[13] However, it is not necessary to resort to 'accidents' as an explanation of the difference between Class A and Class B accounting. It is suggested that the model which is restated in more detail below is powerful enough without this feature. In the end the validity of this claim is an empirical matter.

Summary on excluded factors

Many of the factors which have been examined in this section may be contributory causes to accounting differences or may be *associated* with accounting differences. However, it has been suggested that each can be eliminated as a major reason for the differences identified at the first split of accounting systems into two classes. At lower levels in a classification, many of these factors may be useful explanations of relatively small differences between systems. Further, some of the factors, certainly 'culture', help to explain the different types of capital markets which, according to proposals here, do explain the major groupings.

3.6 A proposed model

The model proposed here consists of a number of linked constructs which will be expressed as propositions. Part of the model can be expressed in simplified form as in Figure 3.2, which amends Doupnik and Salter's proposal (summarised in

| External environment | → | Culture, including institutional structures | → | Strength of equity-outsider system | → | Class of accounting |

Figure 3.2 Simplified model of reasons for international accounting differences (source: author).

Figure 3.1). The variables needed have been introduced in the text above, but now need to be marshalled.

The first variable is the type of country culture and the second is the strength of the equity-outsider financing system. I assume that some cultures lead to strong equity-outsider markets, and others do not. However, this is an issue for economists and others and is not examined in detail here. The point of departure for the constructs and hypotheses explained below is the second variable: the nature of the equity markets. Suggestions have been made here about how empirical researchers could measure this variable, perhaps leading to a 0/1 (weak or strong equity-outsider market) classification.

A further variable is the type of company. For most companies (insider companies), a controlling stake is in the hands of a small number of owners. For a comparatively few companies (outsider companies), control is widely spread amongst a large number of 'outsider' equity-holders. Countries with strong equity-outsider systems generally have a large number of outsider companies which may comprise most of a country's GNP, but other countries may also have a few of these companies.

The fourth variable is the country's degree of cultural self-sufficiency. As discussed earlier, some countries have strong indigenous cultures whereas others have imported cultures which are still dominated or heavily influenced from outside. This dichotomy will be expressed by using the labels CS (for culturally self-sufficient) and CD (for culturally dominated). Researchers might wish to measure this in various ways, for example by the number of decades since a country gained political independence from another. Many developing countries are CD and many developed countries are CS, but there are exceptions. Again, the boundary between CS and CD is not always clear, but researchers should have little difficulty in classifying most countries. Concentration should be placed on aspects of business culture in cases where this may give a different answer from other aspects of culture.

The final variable is the type of financial reporting system (or, in short, 'accounting system') introduced earlier as Class A or Class B. Again, preliminary suggestions have been made about how researchers might measure and classify systems in this way.

The theoretical constructs which link these variables can now be brought together. It is relevant here to repeat the point that more than one accounting system can be used in any particular country at any one time or over time.

The model can be expressed in terms of propositions, which are then explained and illustrated:

P1: The dominant accounting system in a CS country with a strong equity-outsider system is Class A.

P2: The dominant accounting system in a CS country with a weak (or no) equity-outsider system is Class B.

P3: A CD country has an accounting system imported from its dominating country, irrespective of the strength of the CD country's equity-outsider system.

P4: As a country establishes a strong equity-outsider market, its accounting system moves from Class B to Class A.

P5: Outsider companies in countries with weak equity-outsider markets will move to Class A accounting.

The analysis can begin with culturally self-sufficient (CS) countries (Propositions P1 and P2 above), as illustrated in Figure 3.3. For these countries, it is suggested that the class of the dominant accounting system will depend upon the strength of the equity-outsider market (or on its strength in the past, if there is inertia). Strong equity-outsider systems will lead to Class A accounting (see Table 3.5), whereas others will lead to Class B accounting. As explained earlier, the term 'dominant accounting system' is used to refer to the type used by enterprises representing the majority of a country's economic activity. For example, small unlisted enterprises in strong equity market countries might not practise Class A accounting or indeed any financial reporting at all.

Propositions P3 to P5 are now examined. Proposition P3 is that, in culturally dominated (CD) countries, accounting systems are imported. Sometimes a CD country will also have had time to develop the style of equity market associated with the culture. Then, Propositions P1 or P2 will hold as in CS countries. However, sometimes a CD country may have imported its culture and its accounting system without establishing the related equity market. In this case the accounting system will seem inappropriate for the strength or weakness of the equity-outsider financing system. Proposition P4 is that, if either a CS or a CD country with a traditionally weak equity market gradually develops a strong equity-outsider system, a change of accounting towards Class A will follow. Also (P5), in a country with weak equity-outsider markets, there may be *some*

Figure 3.3 Application of Figure 3.2 to culturally self-sufficient countries (source: author).

'outsider companies' (as defined earlier). Commercial pressure will lead these companies towards Class A accounting, even if the dominant system in the country is Class B. For such a company, there will be rewards in terms of lower cost of capital from the production of Class A statements, particularly if there is an international market in the company's shares. If legal constraints hinder movement towards Class A accounting, then the company can use extra disclosures or supplementary statements.

Figure 3.4 shows some aspects of these constructs. The continuous arrows are those from Figure 3.3. Dotted arrows (a) and (c) concern aspects of Proposition P3. Arrow (b) relates to Proposition P4, and Arrow (d) Proposition P5. Some illustrations, which are set in the 1990s before adoption of IFRS by several countries, are:

1   (Arrow a) New Zealand is a CD country with wholesale importation of British culture and institutions (Type 1), including a strong equity-outsider system and Class A accounting. Whether the Class A accounting resulted from the equity market or from direct cultural pressure is not important to the model; it probably arose from both.
2   (Arrow b) China is a country without a strong equity-outsider tradition but which moved towards such a system. Class A accounting followed (Davidson *et al.*, 1996).
3   (Arrow c) Malawi is a CD country with very weak equity markets[14] but where the accountancy profession adopted Class A accounting, consistent with its colonial inheritance from the UK.
4   (Arrow d) The Deutsche Bank, Bayer and Nestlé are companies from countries with traditionally weak equity markets. These companies became interested in world equity-outsider markets, so they adopted Class A accounting for their group accounts.[15]

3.7 Some tests

The above model (as originally proposed in Nobes, 1998) has been applied by several researchers. Two examples are looked at here.

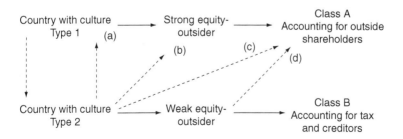

Figure 3.4 A proposed model of reasons for international accounting differences (source: author).

China

Xiao *et al.* (2004) examine proposition P2 (arrow b of Figure 3.4) in the context of China. While agreeing with the basic point of the proposition, they suggest that political factors affected the way in which Class A accounting was adopted.

Germany

Tarca *et al.* (2012) test proposition P5 (arrow d of Figure 3.4) in the context of Germany in 1999 when companies could choose to move from German accounting to IFRS for their consolidated reporting. Tarca *et al.* report 'strong support' for P5.

3.8 Have international differences survived the arrival of IFRS?

There are many ways in which international differences have survived the arrival of IFRS. First, in some major countries (e.g. the USA), IFRS is not allowed, except for foreign companies listed on US exchanges. Second, in some countries, IFRS is not required and is uncommon (e.g. in Japan) or not universal (e.g. in Switzerland). Third, even where IFRS is required for the consolidated statements of listed companies, it is uncommon or not allowed for unconsolidated statements (e.g. most EU countries).

A quite different way in which international differences have survived is that IFRS can be practised differently in different countries. Ball (2006, p. 15) notes, concerning IFRS practice, that 'the incentives of preparers (managers) and enforcers (auditors, courts, regulators, boards, block shareholders, politicians, analysts, rating agencies, the press) remain primarily local'. In other words, IFRS practices might be influenced by the same forces (examined earlier in this chapter) which drove national GAAPs to be different in the first place, such as different tax systems and different prime purposes of accounting, linked to different owners and financiers of companies. For example, a country that has few listed companies with widespread ownership might not need financial reporting that focuses on helping users to predict cash flows and will, instead, tend to align financial reporting with tax calculations. The influence can be indirect. For example, tax considerations could influence a company's accounting policies (e.g. choosing weighted average inventory costing) or estimations (e.g. maximising the size of impairments or provisions) in unconsolidated statements under a national GAAP; and these might flow through to IFRS consolidated statements. Even if such forces are no longer relevant, companies might prefer to continue with previous practices for administrative ease or to provide continuity for users.

Kvaal and Nobes (2010) show that, for five major stock markets (Australia, France, Germany, Spain and the UK), the IFRS practices of large listed companies continue pre-IFRS national traditions. Companies can do this because of flexibility within IFRS. The result is the existence of distinct national profiles of IFRS practices. Kvaal and Nobes (2010) studied 2005/6 financial statements, but

Kvaal and Nobes (2012) confirm the persistence of these national profiles through to 2008/9.

These papers, and this section, consider only 'overt' policy choices that are clearly visible in accounting standards and in the practices of companies. Nobes (2006, 2013) looks at a wider range of issues on which IFRS differences might be found along national lines, including different implementations of IFRS (see Chapter 7), translation problems, different degrees of enforcement and different interpretations.

Chapters 4 to 6 examine classifications of national accounting systems in the pre-IFRS era. Chapter 7 looks at the various ways in which classification remains relevant in the IFRS era.

Notes

1 See, for example, Gonzalo and Gallizo (1992, ch. 3).
2 The idea of 'developed' or 'culturally self-sufficient' is examined further later.
3 Herr Biener of the German Finance Ministry announced this at the board meeting of the International Accounting Standards Committee in Amsterdam in May 1996. In 1998, German law changed in order specifically to allow this.
4 Japan's SEC, its structure of Securities Laws and its stock market owe much to US influence during the occupation following the Second World War.
5 The distinguishing feature of French accounting, the *plan comptable*, was first adopted in France while under German occupation (Standish, 1995).
6 The German accounting plan, though copied in France, was abolished by the occupying Western powers after the Second World War. A version survived in the communist East Germany until reunification.
7 For example, in both the UK and Germany (typical Class A and Class B countries, respectively), there are large numbers of legal cases on the determination of taxable income and some on the determination of distributable income, but there are few or none on the determination of consolidated accounting profit (i.e. cases where there is no tax motivation).
8 This is examined in Nobes and Parker (2012, ch. 2).
9 From observation of Anglo-Saxon countries, it seems that inflation of above 10 per cent for several years will cause a response (e.g. in the UK in the early 1950s or early 1970s), and the same applies to some continental European countries in the 1970s (Tweedie and Whittington, 1984).
10 For example, many South American countries respond with compulsory government-controlled systems of general price level adjusted accounting, whereas English-speaking countries responded with rules written by the profession (although there was government involvement) which required some supplementary disclosures (Tweedie and Whittington, 1984).
11 For example, the Netherlands is often said to have been influenced by the current value theories of Limperg and the German business economist Schmidt (Zeff *et al.*, 1992).
12 For example, see Table 1.11 in Nobes and Parker (2012).
13 This is examined by Nobes (1996), where it is suggested that timing is a key factor. For example, the US requirement to amortise goodwill was introduced earlier than UK standard setting on this issue, when goodwill was far less significant.
14 These issues are discussed by Nobes (1996).
15 For example, Bayer adopted international accounting standards (IASs) for its group accounts for 1994, and Deutsche Bank produced supplementary IAS group accounts for 1995. Nestlé published IAS group accounts.

4 An overview of accounting classifications

4.1 Introduction, purposes

International classification in accounting has been going on for over a century, as will be explained. As in other fields, classification may be used as a way of describing and comparing different accounting systems. The activity involved in preparing a classification should encourage precision. A classifier should be led to examine the exact nature and importance of the differences and similarities between the accounting systems of different countries.

A classification in accounting may also help to shape development rather than merely to describe how things are. For example, classification facilitates the study of the logic of, and of the difficulties facing, harmonisation. Further, by studying a classification, a developing country might be better able to understand the available accounting systems, and which would be most appropriate for its own purposes.

For the teaching of students and for the training of accountants and auditors who move or deal internationally, a classification may prove valuable. For example, US accountants wishing to learn about Belgian domestic accounting rules might usefully start by noting that it is classified with French accounting rather than with Dutch accounting. Such a use may be particularly valuable for those with a peripheral interest in this field who find it hard enough to keep up with accounting in their own countries, without trying to understand accounting elsewhere.

For the profession or legislators in a country, it may be possible to use a classification to predict problems that may have to be faced, and to estimate the most suitable solutions by looking at other countries 'near' to it. It has even been suggested that a way of changing from one accounting system to another may be to adjust the economic and political parameters to those more conducive to the desired system (AAA, 1977). However, this seems like trying to wag a tail by moving the dog.

The next section looks at the lessons learned from other disciplines. The rest of the chapter then provides an overview of the accounting classifications (Section 4.3), and asks how much the classifications merely reflect the classifiers (Section 4.4).

4.2 Lessons from other disciplines

Lessons from other fields (see Chapter 2) can be applied in accounting. First, although judgement is vital, a classification should do more than reflect the mind of the classifier (see Section 4.3). For this, detailed observation is necessary, and this is where judgement must come in.

In chemistry, once ideas of atomic weights and numbers had been established, classification posed few problems. However, in biology the difficulties were and are considerable; and here there are close analogies with comparative accounting. Exactly which criteria should be used to classify and what weights to give them are matters of judgement. Members of a class resemble each other as cousins do, looking alike not because they all have one feature in common but because they all display a number of characteristics from a long list of those appropriate to the family. Judgement is needed to avoid such classifications as Plato's of man as a featherless biped.

David and Brierley (1978), who have classified legal systems, warn us that, for social sciences, the difficulty is great. Their words are of such great relevance to accounting classification that a substantial quotation is here included:

> the diversity of laws does not really reside in the fact that different national laws may on a variety of topics have different rules.... The law of any country will, of course, be concretely manifested at any given time by means of just such a series of rules – the juridical phenomenon which they represent is, however, far more complex. Each law in fact constitutes a *system* ...
>
> When endeavouring to determine the families into which different laws can be grouped, it is preferable to take into consideration these constant elements rather than the less stable rules found in the law at any given moment.... The classification of laws into families should not be made on the basis of the similarity or dissimilarity of any particular legal rules, important as they may be; this is ... inappropriate when highlighting what is truly significant in the characteristics of a given system of law.
>
> (pp. 18–19)

Thus, a classification is by no means theory free. A sensible classification is not produced by a summarisation of a mass of facts. It involves preconceptions, judgments and weightings. Taxonomy is a matter of interpretation: finding the homologues.

Some proposed rules of classification have been summarised by the American Accounting Association (1977, pp. 77–78). Drawing on set theory, four properties were seen as useful. First, the characteristics of a classification should be adhered to consistently. That is, throughout any classification the characteristics used as the means of differentiating one element from another should be the same. If it is the number of feet of an animal, then this should be adhered to. However, different purposes for a classification may of course lead to the use of different characteristics, and in practice it may turn out to be impractical to obey this criterion.

Second, a good classification should contain sufficient subsets to exhaust a given universe. That is, a chemical element, or a plant, or an accounting system should not be unclassifiable due to possessing an extreme amount of a characteristic or to displaying no characteristics which are criteria for classification in the system.

Third, all subsets should be mutually exclusive in such a way that no element may fall into more than one of them. (The discovery of a duck-billed platypus, which lays eggs but suckles its young, necessitates a new group labelled 'monotremes'.) As has been said, recognition of evolution casts some doubt on the practicality of this criterion.

Lastly, hierarchical integrity should be observed. For example, in the Linnaean biological classification, any species of plant or animal is always in the bottom tier of the main ranks of the classification (except, that is, for individuals within a species), always belongs to a *genus*, which belongs to a *family* and so on.

As Roberts (1995) observes, the AAA's desiderata are not necessarily generally supported by the scientific community. However, reference will be made to some of their criteria later.

4.3 An overview of the classifications

Synthesis

Some of the main features of international accounting classifications are summarised in Table 4.1. Several of these classifications (e.g. items 3, 4, 14 and 15 of Table 4.1) relate to influences on accounting rather than to accounting itself. Roberts (1995) calls the former 'extrinsic' and the latter 'intrinsic'; or they could be called deductive and inductive. A classification of the classifications is shown as Figure 4.1.

The rest of this section summarises various aspects of the classifications. Chapter 5 looks in detail at the extrinsic classifications, and Chapter 6 at the

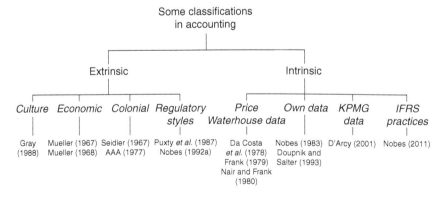

Figure 4.1 A taxonomy of some accounting classifications.

intrinsic ones based on pre-IFRS accounting rules and practices. Chapter 7 examines classification in the IFRS world, including a classification of countries by IFRS practices. Chapter 8 includes a meta-analysis of all the classifications of accounting systems, and asks whether the classifications are anything better than arbitrary.

The range of companies

The scope of the data (e.g. restrictions by sector or listing status) is recorded in column 3 of Table 4.1). As may be seen, most classifications did not specify a scope. This reduces their usefulness, because the practices of listed companies vary from those of unlisted companies; and, even among listed companies, size has a major effect.[1] The last classification in Table 4.1 was the only one to mention sectors. It included companies in all sectors, but displayed the sectoral mix and excluded data on financial companies for topics for which sector-specific practices were anticipated. On such grounds, the exclusion of financial companies is common in much research involving accounting data. However, this creates a different problem: in all countries, the financial sector is significant and, in some (e.g. Australia, Italy, Spain and the UK), it is the most important sector among large listed companies, as shown later. Therefore, exclusion of the sector presents a misleading picture of a whole accounting system.

The importance of sector in influencing accounting policy was first systematically investigated by Jaafar and McLeay (2007), who examined three policy issues for companies from 13 EU countries using national accounting rules, in a pre-IFRS world. Consequently, Jaafar and McLeay were not investigating policy *choices* only but a mixture of different requirements and different choices. They found that country was a much stronger explanatory variable than sector, but that sector had some influence. Apart from the financial sector, which is excluded from many studies on policy choice, a sector which might make idiosyncratic choices is extractives, given the degree to which US practices dominate.[2] Jaafar and McLeay found some evidence of this; and it might be important for countries in which extractive companies constitute a large industry sector (e.g. Canada).

The period measured

The users of classifications should also be aware that countries can change their positions over time.[3] Table 4.1 (column 3) gives information on the dates of the data used for the classifications, noting that most classifiers have not specified a date.

The characteristics and data chosen

The discussions about chemistry, biology and cosmology above showed that the nature and definitions of the characteristics chosen as the basis for classification

Table 4.1 Features of some classifications

1 Researchers	2 No. of countries	3 Range of companies (e.g. sectors, large, listed)	4 Date of data	5 No. of topics	6 Type of data	7 Classification method	8 Classification type
1 Hatfield, 1911	4	Unspecified	Unspecified, c.1910	0	Impressions of practices	Judgement	3 groups
2 Mueller, 1967	5	Unspecified	Unspecified, c.1965	1	Impressions of purposes	Judgement	4 unconnected groups
3 Seidler, 1967	7	Unspecified	Unspecified, c.1965	1	Impressions of influences	Judgement	3 unconnected groups
4 AAA, 1977	6	Unspecified	Unspecified, c.1975	1	Impressions of influences	Judgement	5 unconnected groups
5 da Costa et al., 1978	38	Unspecified	Unspecified, c.1973	100	Mixture of rules and impressions of practices (by Price Waterhouse partners)	PCA	2 unconnected groups
6 Frank, 1979	38	Unspecified	Unspecified, c.1973	233	As above	PCA, MDS	4 unconnected groups
7 Nair and Frank, 1980	38, 46	Unspecified	Unspecified, c.1973 and c.1975	233, 264	As above	PCA, SSA	4/5 unconnected groups for measurement; 7 for disclosure
8 Goodrich, 1982	64	Unspecified	Unspecified, c.1979	26	Impressions of concepts (by Price Waterhouse partners)	PCA	5 unconnected groups
9 Nobes, 1983b	14	Listed	1980	9	Impressions of practices	PCA	Hierarchy of 2 groups, leading to 6 groups

10 Puxty et al., 1987	4	Unspecified	Unspecified, c.1985	3	Impressions of regulatory style	Judgement	Positions of the countries with respect to 3 regulatory ideals
11 Shoenthal, 1989	2	Unspecified	Unspecified, c.1987	1	Impressions of competencies of auditors	Judgement	2 unconnected groups
12 Doupnik and Salter, 1993	50	Economically significant entities	1990	114	Impressions of practices (by academics and auditors)	Average-linkage clustering	Hierarchy of 2 groups, leading to 9 groups
13 d'Arcy, 2001	15	Listed; consolidated and unconsolidated	Unspecified, based on Ordelheide and Semler, 1995	129	Rules	Clustering, MDS	4 groups with MDS
14 Leuz et al., 2003	31	Listed	Based on La Porta et al., 1998	9	Facts and impressions relating to stock markets and investor protection	Clustering by k-means	3 groups in order
15 Leuz, 2010	49	Listed	'2000s'	13	Facts and impressions on legal system, securities regulation	Clustering by k-means	3 groups, then 5 groups
16 Nobes, 2011	8	Large, listed, consolidated, excluding financials for some topics	2008/9	13	Practices	PCA, MDS, clustering	3 groups by PCA; hierarchy starting with 2 groups

Key
PCA = principal component analysis; MDS = multidimensional scaling; SSA = smallest space analysis.

is vital. It is therefore inevitable that classifiers must use judgement in selecting and defining the characteristics used to represent the objects to be classified. This topic is largely an issue for the 'intrinsic' classifications of Table 4.1 (i.e. those that classify countries by their accounting rules/practices rather than by influences on the accounting), so we return to it in Chapters 6 and 7.

The techniques of classification

Table 4.1 (column 7) also shows the techniques used for classification. These range from qualitative assessments to several different statistical methods. The resulting classifications range (see column 8) from lists of apparently unrelated groups of countries to hierarchies (family trees or dendrograms) of related countries. Roberts (1995, p. 649) pointed out the dangers of pushing the evolutionary analogies of the family trees too far. Dendrograms can summarise similarities and differences without invoking evolution. Roberts (p. 656) therefore also questioned the use of such terms as 'species' in an accounting classification. I agree that it is not necessary; the term 'system' serves well enough for a set of individuals with important characteristics in common.

Roberts (p. 652) suggests that analogies with the classification of languages might be more appropriate as languages both converge (they interbreed) and diverge, whereas species only diverge. I accept that, too. However, as discussed earlier, the Linnaean system did not begin as evolutionary but was based on assessing shared characteristics. When evolution was added in (greatly aided later by the analysis of DNA), the broad outline of the animal classification survived although many details were revised. Likewise, although the hierarchical accounting classifications work on the assessment of common characteristics, the inclusion of evolution might lead to similar results. For example, the common ancestor of UK and US accounting could perhaps be traced to nineteenth century UK practice. By contrast, the common ancestor of French and UK accounting lies much further in the past, perhaps in the middle of the sixteenth century.[4] Even use of the apparently scientific word 'species' might not be entirely out of place, given the discussion above about the vagueness of the term in biology.

The statistical methods of classification employed by some classifiers largely relate to the intrinsic classifications (although the extrinsic classifications of Leuz use some of them), so they are outlined in Section 6.1. In principle, these methods are sensitive to which countries are included. For example, a clustering program starts by finding the two nearest countries, showing them together and then treating the average of them as a 'country' for the next stage of clustering. So, exclusion of one country can affect the 'seeding' of the first cluster, which can then affect the position of many other countries. This is investigated in Chapter 8.

4.4 Do the early classifications reflect the classifiers?

As Table 4.1 shows, the early classifications involve no explicit data, so were perhaps especially susceptible to the world views of the classifiers. The discussions of cosmology and anthropology in Chapter 2 showed how susceptible classification can be to the nature of the classifiers. For accounting classifications, most of the early writers had US or UK origins, so they were most familiar with US and UK accounting, and had noticed the differences. They then fitted the rest of the world around that starting point, often leading to a three-way classification: US, UK and other. This explanation is consistent with classifications 1, 3 and 4 of Table 4.1: Hatfield (1911), the identical one of Seidler (1967) and the similar one of the American Accounting Association (AAA, 1977). These classifications were all drawn up by Americans. However, Mueller's initial education was in Germany,[5] so he had a different *Weltanschauung*. Mueller puts the US and the UK together in one class, and has three other classes typified by a different continental European country. This suggests that the nature of the classifiers affected the classifications.

An extreme version of the above approach, of starting with the US and the UK, can be found in Shoenthal (1989) and in Alexander and Archer (2000). In these, the writers (all from North America or the UK) identify some differences between the US and the UK (though these relate to the context of accounting rather than to accounting practices) and then conclude that the US and the UK cannot be classified together. This would be like observing that two cousins exhibit many differences, and therefore cannot be closely related. Nobes (1992a, 2003) points out the problems.

4.5 One country, two systems

The expression 'one country, two systems' was coined to describe Hong Kong when it was returned to China in 1997 after more than 150 years of British rule. For example, Hong Kong retained English law, the Hong Kong dollar and accounting standards (based on UK standards and then international standards).

I appropriate the phrase here to refer to a feature of the 1990s onwards, whereby some countries exhibited two different accounting systems for different purposes. For example, from 1993, a few large German listed companies used US GAAP or International Accounting Standards for consolidated statements but continued to use German national rules for unconsolidated statements. This has been formalised from 2005 whereby IFRS is only required (and only allowed) for consolidated statements in several EU countries.

Consequently, as mentioned in Chapter 3, it no longer made sense to classify *countries* by their accounting, because many countries operated two accounting systems. This was pointed out by Roberts (1995), and the idea appeared in one classification of the late 1990s, as will be seen in Chapter 6.

Notes

1 For example, see Nobes and Perramon (2013).
2 For example, under IFRS, there are no detailed rules on accounting issues associated with extraction.
3 For example, see Nobes (1998).
4 The earliest double-entry bookkeeping records in France and England date from 1299 and 1305, respectively. However, both were isolated examples kept by Italian firms of merchants in versions of Italian. Domestic practice might instead be traced to translations of Pacioli's tractatus on bookkeeping, which were produced in France and England in the middle of the sixteenth century (Comber, 1956; Yamey, 1997).
5 Until moving to California at age 22, and then taking various degrees.

5   Extrinsic classifications

5.1 Introduction

Table 4.1 and Figure 4.1 summarised the accounting classifications, noting that several of them related to influences on accounting. These 'extrinsic' classifications are the subject of this chapter. All of these classifications, until those of Leuz, involved no explicit data. This increases the chance that the classifications reflect the classifiers rather than the phenomena being classified; the problem addressed in Section 4.3.

5.2 Mueller's classifications

In the late 1960s, Professor Gerhard Mueller broke new ground by preparing classifications of 'patterns of development of accounting' (1967) and of 'business environments' (1968). The first of these is a set of four patterns which is not accompanied by an explanation of the methods used to obtain it. However, the 'range of four is considered sufficient to embrace accounting as it is presently known and practised in various parts of the globe' (Mueller, 1968, p. 2). Each group is illustrated by one or two examples. It may well be that it is not reasonable to expect a more sophisticated classification, particularly in a pioneering work, and that Mueller's informed judgement was one of the best methods of classification available.

Mueller stresses that the types of accounting rules which exist in a country are a product of economic, political and other environments, which have determined the nature of the system. This also suggests that other countries' rules would not be appropriate to that country and that rules must be chosen to fit a country's needs. Consequently, doubt is cast on the possibility and usefulness of harmonisation.

Mueller's four groups, which are summarised in a later work (Choi and Mueller, 1978, ch. 2) are:

1   *Accounting within a macroeconomic framework*
    In this case, accounting has developed as an adjunct of national economic policies. We might expect such financial accounting to stress value-added statements, to encourage income-smoothing, to be equivalent to tax accounting and to include social responsibility accounting. Sweden is said to be an example.

2   *The microeconomic approach*

This approach can prosper in a market-oriented economy which has individual private businesses at the core of its economic affairs. The influence of micro-economics has led accounting to try to reflect economic reality in its measurements and valuations. This means that accounting rules must be sophisticated, but flexible. Developments like replacement cost accounting will be accepted most readily in such systems. The Netherlands is suggested as an example.

3   *Accounting as an independent discipline*

Systems of this sort have developed independently of governments or economic theories. Accounting has developed in business, has faced problems when they arrived and has adopted solutions which worked. Theory is held in little regard and turned to only in emergencies or used *ex post* in an attempt to justify practical conclusions. Expressions such as 'generally accepted accounting principles' are typical. Mueller recognises the accounting systems of the United Kingdom and the United States as examples. He is clearly making a similar point, though many years before and for a quite different reason, to Watts and Zimmerman (1979) when they argue that 'no normative theory currently in the accounting literature ... can explain or will be used to justify all accounting standards'. It has also been said that accountancy is 'patron based' and subservient to business interests rather than to theory.

4   *Uniform accounting*

Such systems have developed where governments have used accounting as a part of the administrative control of business. Accounting can be used to measure performance, allocate funds, assess the size of industries and resources, control prices, collect taxation, manipulate sectors of business and so on. It involves standardisation of definitions, measurements and presentations. France is cited as an example.

Mueller was not classifying accounting systems directly, but on the basis of differences in the importance of economic, governmental and business factors in the development of particular systems. However, one might expect that systems which have developed in a similar way would have similar accounting practices. Chapter 3 suggests that the UK and the USA have similar accounting practices; Mueller's developmental classification also puts them together.

Nevertheless, there are a few problems with Mueller's classification. The fact that there are only four exclusive groups and no hierarchy reduces the usefulness of the classification. Thus, the Netherlands is the only country in one of the groups, and the classification does not show whether Dutch accounting is closer to Anglo-Saxon accounting than it is to Swedish accounting. Similarly, the classification cannot include such facts as that German accounting exhibits features which remind one of macroeconomic accounting as well as uniform accounting. Lastly, Russian or communistic accounting is left out entirely. This may, of course, be sensible if the classification is dealing with published financial reporting.

As has been said, the strengths of Mueller's classification are its pioneering nature and that it considers the context and development of accounting systems.

Table 5.1 Business environments classification

Factors:
1   Stages of economic development
2   Stages of business complexity
3   Shades of political persuasion
4   Reliance on some particular system of law

Sets of environments:
 1   United States/Canada/ Netherlands
 2   British Commonwealth (excluding Canada)
 3   Germany/Japan
 4   Continental Europe (excluding Germany, Netherlands, Scandinavia)
 5   Scandinavia
 6   Israel/Mexico
 7   South Africa
 8   The developing nations of Near and Far East
 9   Africa (excluding South Africa)
10   Communist nations

Source: Mueller (1968, pp. 92–95).

Thus, it does not make the mistake of misclassification based on superficial similarities.

Mueller's (1968) second classification is of business environments. He again makes his point that different business environments need different accounting systems and that this should be considered when trying to change or harmonise accounting. Mueller uses estimates of economic development, business complexity, legal system and political and social climate. Ten groupings are identified (see Table 5.1). Although the group comprising 'developing nations of the Near and Far East' might be argued to *need* similar accounting systems, it surely does not have them. Further, the 'Israel and Mexico' group is perhaps an example of man as a featherless biped or of David and Brierley's second criterion being broken. That is, although these countries may have appeared similar at one moment, they have different underlying political, social, geographical, religious and historical factors. Thus, to expect them to continue to react in a similar way for the purposes of accounting or business is to invite disappointment.

5.3 Spheres of influence

There have been some further 'subjective' classifications based on 'spheres of influence'. Seidler (1967) suggested three groups: British, American and continental European. Also, a committee of the American Accounting Association (1977, pp. 105, 129–130) produced a 'zones of influence' classification. The zones are:

1   British
2   Franco-Spanish-Portuguese
3   Germanic-Dutch

4   US
5   communistic.

These zones might equally well have been produced by an historian or a politician. This is not, of course, necessarily a criticism, bearing in mind the importance of context and development to a proper classification. This classification may be useful when examining the accounting practices of developing countries. However, it seems not to be an advance on Mueller's first classification. It adds no hierarchy, for example. Furthermore, it does not take account of the links between UK and US accounting, yet it groups Germanic with Dutch. This seems inappropriate in the light of the material summarised in Chapter 3, and certainly runs counter to Mueller's classification.

5.4 Morphologies

It was noted in the previous chapter that a morphology may help one towards a classification. The stage before a morphology is a one-dimensional list of characteristics deemed relevant for classification. For example, Previts (1975) provides a list of environmental conditions:

1   stability of currency;
2   nature of business ownership;
3   level of management sophistication;
4   size and complexity of businesses;
5   speed of technological and commercial innovation;
6   presence of specific accounting legislation;
7   type of economy and degree of market freedom;
8   growth pattern of the economy;
9   status of accounting education;
10 status of accounting profession;
11 general level of public education;
12 extent of kindred financial knowledge which would require the existence of sophisticated financial reports to the community; and
13 legal and customary structures of business and finance.

A morphology would need at least one more dimension (AAA, 1977, p. 82). For example, that of the American Accounting Association is shown in Table 5.2. Another, by the Buckleys (1974) concerns the method of setting accounting rules, but was not proposed directly for international purposes. It is shown as Table 5.3. Such parameters as the first two of Table 5.2 (political and economic systems) may seem less relevant than actual characteristics of accounting practice. However, one should remember David and Brierley's warning about the importance of underlying structure as opposed to transitory detail. Inclusion of such background factors may help to avoid the 'Israel with Mexico' problem. The AAA's (1977, p. 97) Committee on International Accounting notes that, 'Parameters P1 and P2 are viewed as being pivotal to the type of accounting system which does (or can) emerge.'

Table 5.2 The AAA's morphology for comparative accounting systems

Parameters	States of nature				
	1	*2*	*3*	*4*	*5*
P1 Political system	Traditional oligarchy	Totalitarian oligarchy	Modernising oligarchy	Tutelary democracy	Political democracy
P2 Economic system	Traditional	Market	Planned market	Plan	
P3 Stages of economic development	Traditional society	Pre-take-off	Take-off	Drive to maturity	Mass consumption
	Micro			*Macro*	
P4 Objectives of financial reporting	Investment decisions	Management performance	Social measurement	Sector planning and control	National policy objective
			Private		
P5 Source of, or authority for, standards	Executive degree	Legislative action	Government administrative unit	Public–private consortium	Private
	Public				
P6 Education, training and licensing	Informal	Formal	Informal	Formal	
P7 Enforcement of ethics and standards	Executive	Government administrative unit	Judicial	Private	
P8 Client	Government	Public	Enterprises Public	Private	

Source: American Accounting Association (1977, p. 99).

Table 5.3 A morphology for establishing accounting standards

	Parameters	1	2	3	4	5
A	Principal beneficiary	Government/public sector	Investors/analysts	Capital/credit markets	Management	Accountants
B	Climate	Laissez faire	Uniformity	Circumstantial variables	–	Plebiscite (poll)
C	Rationale	Inductive theoretic	Deductive theoretic	Pragmatic	Authoritarian	–
D	Where authority vests	Private-accounting profession	Private consortium	Public (government)	Quasi-public	–
E	Primary objective	Conformity	Curb abuses	Power	Authority	Abstract theoretic
F	Sociological rationale	Public protection	Public service	Private rights	Profession's welfare	–
G	Impetus	Internal	Regulatory	Societal	–	–

Source: Buckley and Buckley (1974, p. 139).

These two morphologies have not been taken further to produce a classification of similar countries into groups. It is worth noting just how they fit in with the previous discussion on the techniques of classification. The eight parameters in Table 5.2 are an assessment of the most important structural elements in accounting systems. Thus they are to be used as a means of differentiating between systems. The other two stages of judgement involved in classification would be the assignment of weights to these factors, and then the measurement of each country on each of the parameters.

Mueller's classifications and the 'spheres of influence' classifications have not made such parameters explicit, but by implication they must have been (at least subconsciously) present.

5.5 Classifications by Leuz

Leuz *et al.* (2003) and Leuz (2010) provide a classification of countries based on regulatory variables which might affect the quality of accounting, as in Table 5.4. These include large stock market, low ownership concentration, strong rights of outside shareholders and strong legal enforcement. The highest cluster contains Australia, Canada, Singapore, South Africa, the UK and the US; the next contains continental European countries.

Table 5.4 Cluster membership using regulatory variables

Cluster 1	Cluster 2	Cluster 3
Australia	Austria	Argentina
Canada	Belgium	Brazil
Hong Kong	Chile	Colombia
India	Denmark	Ecuador
Ireland	Finland	Egypt
Israel	France	Indonesia
Malaysia	Germany	Jordan
New Zealand	Greece	Kenya
Singapore	Italy	Mexico
South Africa	Japan	Nigeria
Taiwan	Korea (South)	Pakistan
Thailand	Netherlands	Peru
United Kingdom	Norway	Philippines
United States	Portugal	Sri Lanka
	Spain	Turkey
	Sweden	Uruguay
	Switzerland	Venezuela
		Zimbabwe

Source: adapted by the author from Leuz (2010).

6 Intrinsic classifications in a pre-IFRS world

6.1 Introduction

The majority of the classifications in Table 4.1 are 'intrinsic': they attempt to classify countries (or latterly accounting systems) by their accounting rather than by external influences on accounting. An extract from Table 4.1 is shown here as Table 6.1. This chapter concerns these intrinsic classifications, most of which used some form of data and therefore some form of statistical method. The level of sophistication is therefore greatly in excess of that used for classification in some other social sciences, such as economics or politics, as discussed in Chapter 2.

All the classifications in this chapter were drawn up before the widespread use of IFRS, so they are all about national accounting systems. Although these classifications are supposed to be about accounting, it turns out that none of them collects data on actual accounting practices of companies. As will be seen, they use instead, data on accounting rules, or on impressions of practices, or some mixture. There is one further classification (no. 16) which did collect data on accounting practices, but they were IFRS practices. So, this is discussed in Chapter 7.

This section summarises some of the main statistical methods used. The rest of the chapter examines the data and the results of the classifications.

Three statistical methods have been commonly used by the intrinsic classifiers, as follows.

Principal component analysis

Principal component analysis (sometimes called 'factor analysis') processes the data in order to look for 'components' that are selections of practices with different weights that best explain the variance between the objects of study (in this case, countries). Kim and Mueller (1978) and Hutcheson and Sofroniou (1999) set out the procedures.[1] Having identified the components, the approach then focuses on those that explain the greatest variance. In particular, it is common to select those that have eigenvalues greater than one.[2] Then, each country is assigned to the component (after varimax rotation) on which it loads the most.

Table 6.1 Summary of some features of the intrinsic classifications of Table 4.1

Researchers	No. of countries	No. of topics	Type of data	Classification method
1 Hatfield, 1911	4	0	Impressions of practices	Judgement
5 Da Costa et al., 1978	38	100	Mixture of rules and impressions of practices (by PW partners)	PCA
6 Frank, 1979	38	233	As above	PCA, MDS
7 Nair and Frank, 1980	38, 46	233, 264	As above	PCA, SSA
8 Goodrich, 1982	64	26	Impressions of concepts (by PW partners)	PCA
9 Nobes, 1983b	14	9	Impressions of practices	PCA
12 Doupnik and Salter, 1993	50	114	Impressions of practices (by academics and auditors)	Average-linkage clustering
13 D'Arcy, 2001	15	129	Rules	Clustering, MDS
16 Nobes, 2011	8	13	Practices	PCA, MDS, clustering

Key
PCA = principal component analysis; MDS = multidimensional scaling; SSA = smallest space analysis.

Sampling adequacy is checked by the Kaiser–Meyer–Olkin (KMO) measure which can take values of 0 to 1 (Kaiser, 1970). Scores of above 0.5 can be regarded as acceptable (Kaiser, 1974; Hutcheson and Sofroniou, 1999).

Cluster analysis

The process first identifies the congruence in policies between each pair of countries. It identifies the most similar pair. It then fuses these two together as a single unit and looks for the next nearest pairing, and so on. The vertical branching lines rise as each new country is added, showing increasing dissimilarity.

Multidimensional scaling

This method represents data as a configuration of points in two dimensions. It does not automatically produce clusters but gives a graphical representation of the distances between the countries: 'When the data have not been forced into clusters, the observer can assess better whether clusters exist' (Cormack, 1971, p. 340).

Two versions are available: the 'modern' non-metrical solution using two dimensions (Gordon, 1981, ch. 5), and the 'classical' metric solution. A Mardia measure of 'goodness of fit' can show the percentage of the variation which is explained by the two dimensions.

6.2 Classifications based on PW data

The PW surveys

Classifications 5 to 7 of Tables 4.1 and 6.1 are all based on surveys conducted by Price Waterhouse (1973, 1976, 1979, hereafter PW). The surveys contain information on over 200 accounting practices relating to a number of countries. These are scored on an ordinal scale (e.g. from 0 to 5). The three surveys have all been used by at least one researcher. The size of the surveys is shown in Table 6.2. An example of scoring on a practice is shown in Table 6.3.

The Price Waterhouse data were used by each of the researchers as input to various statistical processes, including factor analysis and cluster analysis. As explained above, the former process involves the identification of factors which explain the variance between the countries. These 'factors' are selections of

Table 6.2 Dimensions of Price Waterhouse surveys

	1973	1976	1979
Number of countries	38	46	64
Number of practices	233	264	267
Length of scale	6	7	7

Table 6.3 Practice 93 'inventories'

	6	5	4	3	2	1	0
Argentina				*			
Australia		*					
Bahamas		*					
Belgium		*					
Bermuda		*					
Bolivia				*			
Brazil				*			
Canada			*				
Chile						*	
Colombia			*				
Denmark		*					
Ethiopia		*					
Fiji		*					
France			*				
Germany				*			
Greece				*			
India				*			
Iran				*			
Iraq				*			
Jamaica		*					
Japan				*			
Kenya			*				
Malaysia		*					
Mexico				*			
Netherlands		*					
New Zealand		*					
Nigeria			*				
Norway			*				
Pakistan			*				
Panama		*					
Paraguay				*			
Peru			*				
Philippines			*				
Rep. of Ireland		*					
Rhodesia			*				
Singapore		*					
South Africa			*				
Spain		*					
Sweden		*					
Switzerland			*				
Trinidad		*					
United Kingdom	*						
United States		*					
Uruguay				*			
Venezuela			*				
Zaire				*			

Source: Price Waterhouse (1973, 1976, 1979).

Notes
Cost determined using FIFO.
0=no application; 1=not permitted; 2=not found in practice; 3=minority; 4=about half; 5=majority; 6=required.

practices with different weights which best explain the variance. It may be possible to assign descriptions to these factors by noting the flavour of the mixture of practices in the factors. As will be seen, some researchers have thus been able to label their factors.

The next stage is that a certain number of the most explanatory factors is selected. Then, the 'significant' scores or all the scores on the relevant practices making up the factors are used to calculate the correlations of each country on each factor. It is hoped that clusters of countries will thereby emerge. The reason why some researchers have taken only some factors and only 'significant' scores is that they believe that the resulting greater clarity justifies the loss of some information.

After examining the classifications based on the PW data, we will return to a critique of them in Section 6.3.

Da Costa, Bourgeois and Lawson

Da Costa, Bourgeois and Lawson (1978, hereafter DBL) used the 1973 PW data which scores 38 countries on 233 accounting practices. DBL, however, use only 100 of these, claiming that 'the data base was screened to eliminate practices which were uniform across countries'. Inspection of the survey reveals only three entirely uniform practices. It is perhaps worth noting that the factor analysis section of the SPSS computer package which they were using accepts a maximum of 100 variables (Nie *et al.*, 1974).

The first stage of DBL's analysis found seven independent factors which explained 63 per cent of the sum of the variances of the scores on each practice. A score was then computed for each country on those seven factors for each practice with which the factor showed a 'significant' correlation. The countries were then correlated with each other and a 'Q-analysis' was performed using the correlation matrix. In such analyses, if one or more countries has a high correlation with one factor and with no other then they may reasonably be grouped into a cluster.

The seven factors found by DBL were examined and found to consist of 'recipes' of practices which would be described as follows:

1   degree of financial disclosure;
2   influence of company law on accounting practice;
3   importance of income measurement;
4   strength of conservatism;
5   influence of tax laws;
6   importance of inflation in the environment;
7   orientation towards capital market users.

These factors seem very reasonable as measures of some of the structural differences between the accounting systems of different countries. The clustering process which followed produced two groups (see Table 6.4). Group 2 contained

Table 6.4 Countries grouped on the basis of the association among their financial accounting practices

Countries	Co-efficient with	
	Group 1	Group 2
Group 1; nc = 26		
Japan	0.95	0.28
Philippines	0.94	0.28
Mexico	0.93	0.32
Argentina	0.93	0.32
Germany	0.90	0.42
Chile	0.90	0.41
Bolivia	0.89	0.43
Panama	0.89	0.45
Italy	0.88	0.43
Peru	0.88	0.43
Venezuela	0.88	0.46
Colombia	0.86	0.50
Paraguay	0.86	0.48
United States	0.86	0.05
Pakistan	0.85	0.49
Spain	0.85	0.49
Switzerland	0.84	0.53
Brazil	0.83	0.51
France	0.83	0.53
Uruguay	0.82	0.52
Sweden	0.81	0.59
India	0.81	0.57
Ethiopia	0.81	0.57
Belgium	0.79	0.60
Trinidad	0.76	0.65
Bahamas	0.75	0.65
Group 2; nc = 10		
United Kingdom	0.004	0.98
Eire	0.19	0.96
Rhodesia	0.48	0.87
Singapore	0.50	0.86
South Africa	0.51	0.86
Australia	0.51	0.85
Jamaica	0.54	0.84
Kenya	0.57	0.81
New Zealand	0.62	0.78
Fiji	0.65	0.75

Source: da Costa *et al.* (1978, p. 79).

the UK and nine former members of the British Empire. Group 1 contained the USA, France, Germany, South American countries and all others except the Netherlands and Canada, which were said to be unclassifiable.

At this point, common sense might have intervened and cast doubt on the meaning of a group containing the US and Germany but not Canada. It is not a great surprise that, if one has only two groups and they are headed by the UK and the USA, then Canada will be difficult to classify. However, is 'group 1' a sensible group? Ignoring the Canadian point for the moment, does it enhance our understanding of comparative accounting to have the USA in the same group as Ethiopia but not as the UK? Surely, the paper's conclusion should have been that it had been useful to test the database, that results had been obtained but that something must be wrong with the data or the methodology, or that more stages to the work were needed before it could be usefully interpreted.

However, there was no such caution. The US was said to be 'the country most dissociated from the British model' (p. 80), based on the remarkable (but apparently believed) co-efficient of 0.05 shown in the right-hand column of Table 6.4 which suggests that, of all the countries in the survey, US accounting is much the least like UK accounting. Further, it was concluded that the group containing France, Germany, etc., 'follows the lead of the United States in dissociating themselves from practices common to the British model' (p. 83). It seems highly unlikely that the makers of company and tax laws that governed accounting in France, Germany, Belgium and Italy bore in mind either that they should follow the USA or that they should dissociate themselves from the UK when legislating.

This paper was pioneering and interesting, but it does present an excellent illustration of many of the problems of classification.

Frank

Frank's (1979) paper uses the same data as DBL, performs a broadly similar analysis and then adds a study of whether the results fit with social and economic environmental factors. Frank identifies four groups, as shown in Table 6.5. He cautions us that certain countries bear strong affinities with groups other than their own, and he checks the results with 'multidimensional scaling'. This latter technique avoids the problem which may follow from the 'categorical' scoring. It counts the number of times the scores on practices are the same for each possible pair of countries.

Frank is much more careful than DBL when discussing whether his results are 'correct' or suggesting that previous classifications (e.g. Mueller, 1967) may be wrong. However, he clearly feels that such 'empirical' work is an advance on previous subjectivity, without being concerned with the subjectively collected 'empirical' data. He does not discuss the fact that physical and life scientists do not classify in this way. They judge which factors are structural, and use only measurements of these factors for the differentiation which leads to classification.

Table 6.5 Four-group classification (Frank) 1973 data

Group I	Group II	Group III	Group IV
Australia	Argentina	Belgium	Canada
Bahamas	Bolivia	Colombia	Germany
Ethiopia	Brazil	France	Japan
Eire	Chile	Italy	Mexico
Fiji	India	Spain	Netherlands
Jamaica	Pakistan	Sweden	Panama
Kenya	Paraguay	Switzerland	Philippines
New Zealand	Peru	Venezuela	United States
Rhodesia	Uruguay		
Singapore			
South Africa			
Trinidad and Tobago			
United Kingdom			

Source: Frank (1979, p. 596).

Nevertheless, it must be said that the four-group result looks very sensible compared to the DBL results. In effect, this comes from splitting down DBL's Group I. No doubt this involved the use of a considerable amount of judgement at various stages of the analysis; this is clearly an essential element but one which the various researchers seem rather ashamed of. However, one might still feel concerned about grouping the USA with Germany and Japan, and not with the UK. In a later work involving Frank (discussed below) this problem is resolved by usefully recognising that *disclosure* practices and *measurement* practices are interfering with each other and need to be separated.

Frank's analysis of social, cultural and economic factors generally supports his four-group classification. It supports ideas that 'cultural and economic factors are associated with the particular set of accounting principles and practices used by various countries' (p. 604).

Nair and Frank

Perhaps the most attractive results, as far as concerns those factors which the present author considers as fundamental and structural, are those of Nair and Frank (1980) when dealing with accounting measurement practices. In this paper, the exercise of judgement is seen more clearly. Both the 1973 and the 1975 surveys are used, but split into those practices concerned with disclosure and those with measurement. This decision, and the resulting difference in the groups, strongly confirms the point that Price Waterhouse's subjectivity in choosing the questions is a vital factor to be considered when processing the data.

The 1973 groupings on measurement practices are shown in Table 6.6. These groupings were produced by using a varimax rotation procedure with the five factors which explained most of the variance (those with eigenvalues exceeding

Table 6.6 Four-group 'measurement' (Nair and Frank) 1973

Group I	Group II	Group III	Group IV
Australia	Argentina	Belgium	Canada
Bahamas	Bolivia	France	Japan
Fiji	Brazil	Germany	Mexico
Jamaica	Chile	Italy	Panama
Kenya	Colombia	Spain	Philippines
Netherlands	Ethiopia	Sweden	United States
New Zealand	India	Switzerland	
Pakistan	Paraguay	Venezuela	
Republic of Ireland	Peru		
Rhodesia	Uruguay		
Singapore			
South Africa			
Trinidad and Tobago			
United Kingdom			

Source: Nair and Frank (1980, p. 429).

1.0, explaining 71 per cent of the variance between them). This procedure associates each country with a single factor. No country had its highest loading on the fifth factor.

What clearly emerge are four very plausible groups. These bear a similarity to those of Frank using the whole 1973 survey. However, the differences between them (compare Tables 6.5 and 6.6) are very interesting. The Netherlands has moved into the UK group which, apart from the former's experimentation with replacement cost and even more 'judgemental' accounting, seems quite reasonable. Germany has moved into a continental European group, leaving behind a US group which is now very credible. Germany's detailed disclosure requirements are no longer confused with its measurement practices, which are importantly different from those of the USA. Group II contains mostly South American countries, many of which were then using some form of general purchasing power accounting.

These results were found to be stable by using the 1975 data. Only a few countries change their groups. This could have been a result of adding extra countries, or of a real change in the accounting practices of these few countries. In the case of Venezuela, which moves from Group III to Group IV, it seems plausible that increasing industrial development and influence of multinational companies explains this. In the case of Pakistan, which moves from Group I to Group II, important political and social changes in the 1970s may explain this. As in Frank's 1979 paper, the social and environmental tests are performed, this time on the 1975 data. Similar supporting evidence about their importance is found.

As for the classification of disclosure practices, it is noted that 'the disclosure practices do not seem to conform to any such conceptual classification schemes. They present a different picture of greater diversity where the boundary lines between different groups become blurred and indistinct.'

For measurement practices, with which the writer is more concerned, Table 6.6 represents an intuitively appealing result. It suggests that, despite all the fears, the data and the methodology are good enough. Perhaps Price Waterhouse turns out to have asked the questions which do reveal the underlying measurement practices, once the interference from the disclosure practices has been removed. Perhaps any 'hard' errors are unbiased and unimportant. Also, too, it seems likely that Nair and Frank used considerable judgement in the exact methods of choosing groups. They also note that their results are 'intuitively appealing' (p. 429), giving the game away that they did expect or hope to confirm the ideas of Seidler, Previts and so on (see Chapter 5) whom they begin with.

Despite this, they still make a statement which might be considered to overplay their hand when they describe the research as 'aimed at empirically assessing the validity of international classifications proposed repeatedly in the accounting literature' (p. 449). It is really we and those earlier researchers (and, I suspect, Nair and Frank) who assess the validity of this new classification in the light of our feeling for the underlying structures in comparative accounting. To some extent they do acknowledge this by noting that 'Since the affiliation of a given country with others is dependent upon the set of accounting practices selected, the validity of cross-country comparisons depends upon the nature of the practice on which the comparison is made' (p. 449).

Here they were particularly referring to the difference between the measurement and the disclosure domains, but it must of course also apply to the selection of measurement practices. That being the case, the usefulness of the PW survey was not that it avoided subjectivity but that it had already been carried out. It would be just as empirical and far more relevant (but much more time consuming) to judge which factors are important for differentiation and to go out and measure them personally in each country.

A real empirical *test* of the classification, as opposed to the *generation* of it, might be to study whether the four different groups react in four different internally homogeneous ways to certain stimuli, such as rapid inflation.

Goodrich

Goodrich (1982) applies factor analysis to the parts of the PW (1979) survey that concern accounting concepts. He detects five groupings, each headed by a prototype country: USA, Switzerland, UK, Brazil and Jersey. The Jersey group contains Germany, the Netherlands, Italy, Senegal and Ecuador. The fact that Goodrich takes such a group seriously (p. 57) is the best illustration imaginable of the pitfalls of the 'empirical' method. It is hard to trust a classification that puts Australia in the same group as Japan and Columbia, and not with the UK and New Zealand. Further discussion followed in Goodrich (1983) and Nobes (1983a).

6.3 Criticisms of the use of the PW data

There are several ways in which the *use* of PW data for the purpose of classification might be criticised. There are also some ways in which the data per se may be reasonably questioned. The former are clearly not the fault of Price Waterhouse, to whom we should be grateful for the enormous effort involved in compiling this rich source of data. However, taken together, these problems are of great significance.

Suitability for purpose

The surveys were not intended as a source of data for classification. They were thus biased towards practical detail rather than fundamental, lasting structure. The PW surveys had begun as a list of differences between US and UK accounting. They therefore did not ask (about a country) such important questions as: (i) are depreciation expenses determined by tax rules? or (ii) is deferred tax accounted for? They asked instead such peripheral questions as whether or not self-insurance provisions were maintained in an internal account by systematic charges to income (PW, 1973, Question 124), which was known to be a topic of US/UK difference.

Further, since the computer sees all characteristics as having equal weight, the mix of questions may add an overwhelming background noise to any important theme that the questions have correctly identified. As an example of this, let us take the three questions on consolidation in the 1973 survey, as shown in Table 6.7. The essential difference between the systems was not clearly shown by considering all three questions with equal weight. The vital question is the third, question 16, which separates out France (at the time) from the other countries shown. Also, the computer might notice that the UK seemed to fit with Germany rather than with the USA. This would be misleading, because the computer had not been told that German companies usually excluded foreign subsidiaries and had a different concept of the 'group'. Questions 14 and 15 are of considerable interest to a practitioner but are quite unimportant for classification, compared to a more structural question such as question 16.

Given the original purpose of the PW data, it is not surprising that they showed the US and the UK as the most different[3] of any pairing of the 36 countries

Table 6.7 1973 survey questions on consolidation for four countries

Practice no.		US	UK	France	W. Germany
14	Consolidated statements *only*	4	1	2	1
15	Consolidated and parent statements	1	5	2	5
16	Parent statements *only*	1	1	4	1

Note
1=not permitted or not found; 2=minority practice; 3=followed by half of companies; 4=majority practice; 5=required.

examined for 1973. Consequently, by using these data, da Costa *et al.* (1978) found again, like Hatfield, that the world had three types of country: US led, UK led, and unclassifiable (i.e. Canada and the Netherlands). Frank (1979) and Nair and Frank (1980) identified four groups from the same data, two of which were those dominated by the US and UK, respectively. Goodrich (1982) used the 1979 PW data and identified five groups, two of which were headed by the US and the UK, though there is another headed by Jersey which (remarkably, as noted earlier) also contains Guatemala, Germany, Italy, the Netherlands and Zaire.

A mixed measurement system

As Table 6.3 shows, the seven-point measurement scale used in the PW survey mixes rules (1 = not permitted; 6 = required) with practices (2 = not found in practice, 5 = majority). Of course, the practices were not empirically measured but based on the opinions of PW partners, relating to an unspecified set of companies. As a result, the scoring system is somewhat incoherent.

Misleading cases

There are important examples of scores on practices which may be seen as correct when the context is carefully examined, but which must be misleading when fed into a computer program. Table 6.8 gives the example of conservatism for the four countries in Table 6.8. It is true that 'prudence' was enshrined in US and UK accounting statements (APB Statement 4 and SSAP 2). It may also have been true that 'conservatism' was not mentioned in French law as such. Thus, the survey may be 'correct' in its scoring on practice no. 11, by its own definition of 'required'. However, the conservatism found in France and Germany is reckoned by those familiar with it to have been of a totally different (and higher) order from that used in the USA and the UK. On this fundamental point, the computer will be misled. As it turns out, practice no. 34 which is also shown in Table 6.8 seems to correspond more with expectations, though there must have been difficulty in standardising the world-wide scoring on 'over-conservatism', as a German accountant's view might be very different from a British accountant's.

Turning to the 1979 survey (effective date: 1 January 1979), another example of the possibility of being misled is the treatment of international accounting standards and other 'requirements'. Taking consolidation, the survey reports

Table 6.8 1973 survey questions on conservatism

Practice no.		US	UK	France	W. Germany
11	Conservatism	5	5	4	5
34	Over-conservative asset valuation	2	1	4	3

Note
Scores as for Table 6.7.

that, for question 209 ('consolidated statements … are prepared for the share-holders'), the answer is 'required' in France. The reason given for this is that the *Commission des Opérations de Bourse* (COB) 'requires' consolidation. In fact, as the annual reports of COB show, only 305 companies published consolidated balance sheets and profit and loss accounts in 1979. This was less than half of the listed companies and a very small proportion of 'enterprises which issue their statements to the general public' about which the survey was said to be (Price Waterhouse, 1979, p. 5).

Further, one wonders whether consolidation practices in Fiji, Malaysia or Trinidad were really correctly understood by suggestions in various survey questions that IAS 3 was being followed. The survey's introduction (pp. 8, 9) sounds a note of caution here, but that was not fed into the computer.

These are examples which could be replicated many times over. A related point is made for one particular country by Zeff (1979, p. 59) who conjectures that 'the Price Waterhouse surveys reported chiefly on the New Zealand subsidiaries of overseas-based corporations, rather than on domestic New Zealand companies'.

Errors

There are also examples of what do seem to be 'hard' errors. These are clearly inevitable in a massive undertaking such as the PW surveys. Table 6.9 shows some extracts from the 1973 and 1976 surveys relating to the UK. Doubt is thereby cast upon the reliability of answers for Bolivia.

Table 6.9 Survey answers for the UK

Practice	Number and score	
	1973	*1976*
A 'Land is shown separately from other fixed assets' *Comment*: It was normally unseparated from buildings	77 required	40 required
B 'Cost of inventories is determined by FIFO' 'Cost of inventories is determined by weighted average' 'Cost of inventories is determined by retail inventory' *Comment*: SSAP 9 specifically allows all three (appendix, paras 11–14)		93 required 95 not permitted 98 not permitted
C There are several examples where UK practice is said to differ from Irish practice in 1976, yet where the countries used identical standards on the subject, e.g. 205		
D 'Leases are capitalized by the lessee' *Comment*: This was not the case in 1973 or 1976.	178 majority	47 majority

Conclusion on the use of PW data

These problems with the data should reinforce the points in Section 6.2 about the need for judgement and theoretical input. Since the data are not perfect and were not designed for the work in hand, it should be clear that they needed to be handled with care. Further, the results from using the data must be treated with caution. As has been seen in the preceding review of the work of other research-ers, it appears that such caution has not always been present. However, Nair and Frank (1980, p. 445) note 'the companies whose practices are reported on in the survey may not all meet the same criteria such as being listed on a stock exchange, or even being publicly held'. The reverse problem has also been noted earlier in this chapter: for example, that some scores are descriptions of the prac-tice of only important listed companies in some countries but of all companies in other countries (e.g. France and consolidation in the 1979/80 survey). This seems of considerable importance but is difficult to correct for when dealing with a vast mass of characteristics and countries.

6.4 An hierarchical classification

One of the shortcomings of the groups shown in all the above classifications is that there is no hierarchy: for example, are the US and UK groups of Frank reasonably close to each other, compared to the continental European group?

Nobes (1983b) set out to solve this problem, and to be precise about the com-panies covered (i.e. listed), the characteristics assessed (i.e. measurement practices) and the date (i.e. 1980). He chose to classify 14 countries, partly on the basis of his knowledge of their accounting practices. Then, deliberately using judgement, Nobes (1983b) sets out nine factors as key differences between accounting systems (see Table 6.10) and a morphology to go with them (see Table 6.11). These were then scored, after collecting data from publications and interviews of audit firms (see Table 6.12). Detailed justifications for the scores were given in Nobes (1992b).

A very clear split of countries into two groups emerges when these scores are totalled, as in Table 6.13. Using a variety of statistical clustering techniques, the four groups in Table 6.14 emerge. Nobes (1983b) had already proposed a hypo-thetical classification based on influences, shown here as Figure 6.1. The results in Tables 6.13 and 6.14 support this.

In the previous editions of this book (Nobes, 1984, 1992b), a far more exten-sive list of countries is classified on a judgemental basis, reproduced in this book as Appendix II. This was copied without attribution by Berry (1987).

It must be admitted that there are two obvious problems with the methods in Nobes (1983b). First, the factors in Table 6.10 are a mixture of influences and practice-related issues. Second, the scoring was subjective (though based on extensive research) and did not involve measuring the practices of real com-panies. Nevertheless, Figure 6.1 has found its way into many textbooks and aca-demic papers (e.g. Roberts *et al.*, 2008, p. 227; Radebaugh *et al.*, 2006, pp. 38, 39; Doupnik and Perera, 2009, p. 38).

Table 6.10 Factors of differentiation

Factor no. (and abbreviation)	Factor name
1 (USER)	Type of users of the published accounts of the listed companies
2 (LAW)	Degree to which law or standards prescribe in detail, and exclude judgement
3 (TAX)	Importance of tax rules in measurement
4 (PRU)	Conservatism/prudence (e.g. valuation of buildings, stocks, debtors)
5 (HC)	Strictness of application of historical cost (in the historical cost accounts)
6 (RC)	Susceptibility to replacement cost adjustments in main or supplementary accounts
7 (CONS)	Consolidation
8 (PROV)	Ability to be generous with provisions (as opposed to reserves) and to smooth income
9 (UNI)	Uniformity between companies in application of rules

Doupnik and Salter (1993) tested the Nobes classification of Figure 6.1 using their own assessments of 114 of PW's accounting topics, based on the impressions of auditors in 50 countries. One of the problems with this is that the data used to 'test' the 1980 classification relate to ten years after it. Nevertheless, Doupnik and Salter confirm all the major features of Figure 6.1.

In a critique of previous classifications, Roberts (1995) suggested that the objects being classified should be 'accounting systems' rather than countries. This became especially important when IFRS began to be used for certain purposes in certain countries (see Section 3.8). Nobes (1998) responded to this with the classification shown here as Figure 6.2. For example, the system 'US GAAP' means the well-defined set of practices (at a particular date) required by US regulators to be used by listed US companies. Examples of users of the system are SEC-registered US companies, and some large Japanese companies for their group statements. The figure suggests that 'US GAAP' bears a family resemblance to UK and IFRS rules (see Chapter 3), and is in a class of systems suited to strong equity markets.

6.5 D'Arcy uses KPMG data

Many years after the PW surveys, a new source of data from a big audit firm became available. This was *Transnational Accounting* produced in two editions by Ordelheide and KPMG (1995, 2001). An abstract of the first edition, in tabular form covering 129 topics of 15 GAAPs (14 countries and the IASC), was published as Ordelheide and Semler (1995). Unlike PW data, which was an

Table 6.11 Morphology based on Table 6.10

Factor	0	1	2	3
1 (USER)	Banks, revenue	–	Institutions	Individuals
2 (LAW)	Detailed prescription	–	–	Lack of prescriptions, much room for judgement
3 (TAX)	Nearly all figs determined	–	–	No figures determined
4 (PRU)	Heavy conservatism	–	–	Dominance of accruals
5 (HC)	No exceptions	–	–	Many exceptions used, considered for all
6 (RC)	No susceptibility	Small experimentation	Supplementary	–
7 (CONS)	Rare consolidation	Some consolidation	Domestic subsids	All subsids + assocs
8 (PROV)	Considerable flexibility	–	–	No room for smoothing
9 (UNI)	Compulsory accounting plan	–	–	No standardized format, rules or definitions

Table 6.12 Scoring based on Table 6.11

	Australia	Belgium	Canada	France	Germany	Italy	Japan	Netherlands	New Zealand	Rep. of Ireland	Spain	Sweden	UK	USA
1 (USER)	3	1	3	1	0	1	0	2	3	2	1	0	2	3
2 (LAW)	3	1	2	1	0	1	1	3	3	2	1	1	2	1
3 (TAX)	3	0	3	0	0	1	0	3	3	3	1	0	3	2
4 (PRU)	2	0	2	0	0	0	0	3	2	2	0	0	2	2
5 (HC)	2	1	1	1	0	0	0	3	2	3	1	0	3	1
6 (RC)	2	1	2	1	0	0	0	2	2	2	0	1	2	2
7 (CONS)	3	1	3	1	1	1	0	2	2	2	1	0	2	3
8 (PROV)	2	1	2	1	1	1	0	2	2	2	1	0	2	3
9 (UNI)	3	0	3	0	1	2	1	3	3	3	0	1	3	3

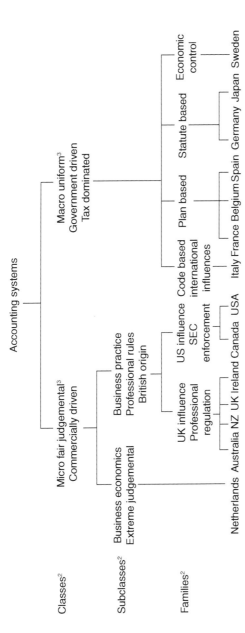

Figure 6.1 A suggested classification of accounting 'systems' in some developed Western countries in 1980 (source: Nobes, 1983b).

Notes
1 This is an abbreviated term for corporate financial reporting.
2 These terms, borrowed from biology, should be interpreted merely as loose labels.
3 The terms at branching points are labels to be used as shorthand to try to capture some of the attributes of the members of the accounting systems below them. This classification has been prepared by a UK researcher and may contain usage of terms that will mislead those from other cultures.

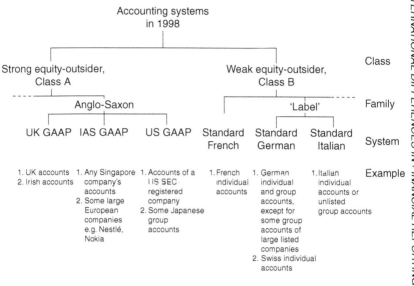

Figure 6.2 Extract from proposed scheme for classification.

Table 6.13 Totals from Table 6.12

	Practices	*Explanatory*
Netherlands	20	8
United Kingdom	18	7
Rep. of Ireland	18	7
Australia	17	9
New Zealand	17	9
Canada	16	8
United States	16	6
France	4	2
Italy	4	3
Belgium	4	2
Sweden	4	1
Germany	4	0
Spain	3	3
Japan	2	1

Table 6.14 Four-group clustering by 'furthest neighbour'

1	*2*	*3*	*4*
Australia	Netherlands	Belgium	Germany
Canada	Ireland	France	Japan
New Zealand	UK	Italy	Sweden
USA		Spain	

incoherent mixture of rules and impressions of practices, the Ordelheide and Semler data concern rules only.

D'Arcy (2001, whose former name was Semler) applies statistical techniques similar to those used by the earlier researchers in this chapter, particularly clustering and multidimensional scaling. From this, d'Arcy concludes that there is a core continental European cluster (Germany, Austria, France and Belgium) and a North American cluster (Canada, US and IASC). However, the two interesting findings are that there is no Anglo-American cluster and that Australia does not fit at all, having 'an outsider position' (p. 345). Just as one should be sceptical about a classification which shows the US and the UK as entirely unrelated (see Section 6.2 on da Costa *et al.*), one should be worried by these two findings of d'Arcy. Is there anything about the data which should concern us?

The usefulness of data relating to rules alone can be questioned. For example, IFRS (IAS 38, para. 72) allows certain intangible assets to be measured at fair value rather than on a cost basis, whereas German and US GAAPs require a cost basis. However, this difference in rules is of doubtful significance if no IFRS companies choose fair value to measure intangibles, which is the case in the sample of German and UK companies of Christensen and Nikolaev (2013). It is surely more significant, for example, that the majority of IFRS-using UK companies choose fair value for investment properties whereas no IFRS-using German companies do,[4] even though all the companies from both countries are using identical rules. In the context of the EU in the 1990s, company law had been harmonised much more than accounting practice had been. This might explain why the UK could not easily be separated from other European countries in the data.

Concerning Australia, the strange result can be explained by poor data. Nobes (2004) focuses on d'Arcy's scores for Australia, the UK and the US. For example, for the section on 'Liabilities and provisions' in Ordelheide and KPMG (1995), most country authors took 'provisions' to refer to items shown on the liabilities side of the balance sheet. However, the Australian contributor discussed only a quite different meaning of provision: allowances against assets, i.e. impairments (p. 130). In Ordelheide and Semler (1995, p. 14), this is picked up as though Australian companies are required to show depreciation provisions as liabilities on balance sheets, and several other errors follow (see Nobes, 2004, Appendix 1, topics 3 to 6). If this and the other data problems were corrected, the conclusion is that the US and the UK would be seen together and that Australia would not be an outlier.

6.6 Summary of intrinsic classifications

The intrinsic accounting classifications in the pre-IFRS era date from 1911 to 2001. Some show highly implausible results. Apart from the earliest one, all the classifications use data and statistical classification techniques. A key issue concerns the type and quality of the data used to measure the characteristics of each country/system. This is summarised in Table 6.1.

Clearly, classifications which used no data (such as the early intrinsic and extrinsic ones up to the 1970s) are less satisfactory than detailed observation of practices. In the non-accounting fields reviewed earlier, the quality of data for classification improved over time in various ways. For accounting research, the annual reports of hundreds of listed companies can now be collected quickly, and many are available in English.[5] By contrast, in the 1960s and 1970s, if the US researchers had wanted to collect the financial statements of all the members of the main French stock market index (for example), that would have proved very difficult, and many of the reports would not have been in English. This might be what held back researchers from detailed observation, but a more likely explanation is that accounting researchers were not yet accustomed to an empirical approach (Watts and Zimmerman, 1979).

Unfortunately, when the era of data arrived, the data used were not very suitable. Data which mix rules and impressions of practices (classifications 5 to 8 and 12) or influences and impressions of practices (classification 9) lack coherence. Data on rules alone (classification 13) are of doubtful relevance. None of the classifications was based on the collection of data relating to the accounting practices of actual companies.

Any of the methods of measuring the characteristics chosen for classification can involve error. As discussed earlier, the PW data used for classifications 5 to 8 certainly contain errors, and the data based on KPMG information (used for classification 13) also produces erroneous scores.

Notes

1 For a useful explanation, see: www.faculty.chass.ncsu.edu/garson/PA765/factor.htm (accessed 4 April 2010).
2 Eigenvalues are a set of scalars associated with a linear system of equations (i.e. a matrix equation). They are also known as quadratic roots, characteristic values, proper values or latent roots.
3 See Exhibit 1 of da Costa *et al.* (1978).
4 In the companies comprising the main German and UK stock market indices (Kvaal and Nobes, 2010).
5 Nobes and Perramon (2013) find that English language reports contain the same information as the originals.

7 Classification in the IFRS era

7.1 Introduction

This chapter investigates international differences in the way in which countries and companies have responded to International Financial Reporting Standards (IFRS). At the country level, some (e.g. South Africa) have adopted IFRS for the consolidated reporting of listed companies, some have made a special national version for such reporting (e.g. Australia). These countries allow IFRS for other purposes. However, some have required it for some purposes but not allowed it for others (e.g. France), while some have not yet allowed it for any purpose, except for foreign companies (e.g. the USA). Where domestic accounting survives for at least some purposes, some countries are converging their domestic accounting with IFRS (e.g. the UK and the USA), while others are making few such changes (e.g. France). Some countries have converged national accounting with IFRS but only for some reporting entities (e.g. China for listed companies). At the company level, there are many differences of practice within IFRS, and specific national versions of IFRS practice are emerging, reminding one of the classifications in Chapter 6. As a result of all this, global comparability (particularly for listed companies) has been improved by the arrival of IFRS, but there is still a long way to go.

There are many ways in which classification might still be helpful in the IFRS era. First, in many countries that have adopted IFRS for consolidated reporting by listed companies, the rest of accounting (the great bulk of it) nevertheless continues under national rules. These national systems continue to differ and can be classified as before. That is, if a particular classification from Chapters 5 or 6 is plausible and up to date, it can still be used.

A new way in which countries can be classified is in their responses to IFRS, in particular the degree to which national regulators allow or require IFRS for various purposes. Section 7.2 investigates this for several major countries. Then Section 7.3 looks at three ways in which the classifications of Chapter 6 might help to predict national responses to IFRS, focusing on Europe. Lastly, different national versions of IFRS practice are emerging, and these can perhaps be classified. Section 7.4 looks at this.

7.2 Classification of countries by ways of implementing IFRS

Introduction to this section

Angus Thomson of the Australian Accounting Standards Board (AASB) stated that: 'Australia definitely adopts IFRSs' (Thomson, 2009, p. 153). This was in response to Nobes (2008, p. 283) who wrote that: 'Australia has chosen not to "adopt" IFRS, but to converge its standards with IFRS.' The distinction has major legal and political aspects. It can affect preparers, auditors and users. This section examines the meaning of 'adoption of IFRS' in the context of jurisdictions. It is based on Zeff and Nobes (2010).

A starting point for discussing the approach of *jurisdictions* to IFRS is that the International Accounting Standards Board (IASB) has no authority of its own to impose accounting standards. This feature is shared with the generality of standard setters, including the Financial Accounting Standards Board (FASB) of the United States. A set of standards (e.g. IFRS) can be accepted into a jurisdiction by several different methods: adopting the standard setter's process, rubber-stamping each standard, endorsing them (with the possibility of some differences), fully converging national standards, partially doing so or merely *allowing* use of the IASB's standards. We now examine these methods.

Adopting the process

The debate about adopting the process was key at an earlier stage of international standardisation. In the 1990s, the International Accounting Standards Committee (IASC) put great efforts into trying to persuade the International Organization of Securities Commissions (IOSCO) to endorse international standards by adopting the IASC's process rather than by examining its standards one-by-one (Kirsch, 2006, p. 293; Camfferman and Zeff, 2007, pp. 323–324).

The simplest way for regulators to use standards is for them to accept that a particular standard *setter* has suitable expertise and independence for its output to be legally imposed upon a class of entities. That is, the regulator can adopt a *process* of standard setting and, therefore, automatically adopt the standards that are produced by the process. There is then no need for individual standards or amendments to be given regulatory approval. Of course, the regulator could later change its mind, and it could seek to influence the development of a particular standard, as many other parties do.

This method of adopting the process is used in the USA and the UK for domestic standards. That is, the Securities and Exchange Commission (SEC) requires its US registrants to follow the FASB's standards. In its Accounting Series Release 150, issued in 1973, the SEC states:

> In meeting this statutory responsibility effectively, in recognition of the expertise, energy and resources of the accounting profession, and without abdicating its responsibilities, the Commission has historically looked to the

standard-setting bodies designated by the profession to provide leadership in establishing and improving accounting principles. The determinations by these bodies have been regarded by the Commission, with minor exceptions, as being responsive to the needs of investors.

The body presently designated by the Council of the American Institute of Certified Public Accountants (AICPA) to establish accounting principles is the Financial Accounting Standards Board (FASB).... [T]he Commission intends to continue its policy of looking to the private sector for leadership in establishing and improving accounting principles...

...For purposes of this policy, principles, standards and practices promulgated by the FASB in its Statements and Interpretations will be considered by the Commission as having substantial authoritative support, and those contrary to such FASB promulgations will be considered to have no such support [footnote omitted].

Somewhat similarly, the Companies Acts in the UK refer to standards as issued by a standard setter. For example: 'In this Part "accounting standards" means statements of standard accounting practice issued by such body or bodies as may be prescribed by regulations' (S.464, Companies Act 2006). So, a standard issued by the Financial Reporting Council needs no further regulatory action. These standards are still allowed in the UK for reporting other than for the consolidated statements of listed companies.

We have not been able to identify many countries that have used this method to adopt IFRS. We note the cases of Australia and Canada later, but conclude that those countries do not exactly fit the description. However, in Israel, the Securities Law refers to Israeli accounting standards, and Standard No. 29 of 2006 requires the use of IFRS as issued by the IASB for listed companies. Standard 29 implies that future amendments to IFRS are automatically adopted.[1]

In South Africa, the arrangements are now somewhat complex. However, for listed companies, the Johannesburg Stock Exchange requires the use of IFRS as issued by the IASB. That instruction is allowed by law to override any other accounting requirements of the Companies Act. So, for listed companies, South Africa has 'adopted the process'.

We must now acknowledge a potential difficulty for many jurisdictions: language. Let us take the example of Rubovia, a country that decides that it would like to adopt IFRS by passing a law requiring companies to follow IFRS as issued by the IASB. There would be no endorsement process (see below), and certainly no deliberate changes to IFRS. However, the Rubovians are generally unsullied by a knowledge of English. So, the Rubovian law refers to 'IFRS as issued by the IASB, as translated into Rubovian'.

The translation process takes several months. So, for example, IFRS 9 (issued by the IASB in November 2009) could have been used by Israeli companies for 2009 annual reports but not by Rubovian companies. Would one still say that Rubovia had adopted IFRS? Yes, probably. Suppose, further, that the Rubovian governmental translators make a few errors.[2] Has Rubovia still adopted IFRS?

Other ways of implementing IFRS

If a jurisdiction is unwilling or unable (for reasons of practicality) to adopt the process, there are several other possible methods of implementing IFRS. However, anything other than adopting the process requires continual action by regulators because the IASB (including the International Financial Reporting Interpretations Committee) changes the content of IFRS nearly every month. Therefore, all the methods below open up possibilities for differences from IFRS as issued by the IASB. At the very least, delays occur in making IFRS available for use by entities.

Two general questions arise. First, can any of these methods be called 'adopting IFRS'? Second, what is the effect of the various methods of implementation on compliance by companies with IFRS as issued by the IASB: is it assured, possible or unlikely? We address these questions after examining the methods.

Rubber stamping in the private sector

For technical or legal reasons, it might be efficient for a jurisdiction to establish a method whereby all the IASB's output is quickly and almost automatically inserted into law without change. This was the approach of Canada for its 2011 implementation.[3] Canada's tradition is that the national and provincial laws refer to the *Handbook* of the Canadian Institute of Chartered Accountants (CICA). The *Handbook* contains accounting standards, in both English and French.[4] The Canadian Securities Administrators intend that CICA's Accounting Standards Committee will make no changes (apart from translation) to 'IFRS as issued by the IASB' before it is inserted into the *Handbook*.

Standard-by-standard endorsement by public authorities

A particularly cumbersome method of implementing IFRS is used in the European Union. Regulation 1606/2002 requires listed companies, when preparing consolidated statements, to use the 'endorsed' versions of international standards that are appended to the Regulation. So, the standards and interpretations in force in 2002 were gradually endorsed, and all subsequent amendments need to be endorsed. Not counting all the bodies that are informally involved (e.g. FEE, the *Fédération des experts comptables européens*), the endorsement process requires action from the European Financial Reporting Advisory Group (EFRAG), the Accounting Regulatory Committee, the Standards Advice Review Group, the European Commission, the European Parliament and, conceivably, even the Council of Ministers.[5]

As a result, individual pieces of the content of IFRS have implementation dates (at least for voluntary adoption) that are different from IFRS as issued by the IASB,[6] and parts of IFRS can be deleted (e.g. as in the case of the 'carve-out' from IAS 39; Whittington, 2005; Zeff, 2010). There are other, more complex, anomalies.[7]

Uncertainty can also be added. For example, IFRS 9 (Financial Instruments) was issued by the IASB in November 2009. EFRAG issued fast-track preliminary advice in favour of endorsement, but the Commission asked for the advice to be withdrawn, and made it clear that IFRS 9 would not be endorsed quickly, if at all.[8]

The resulting EU package of standards is not to be referred to as IFRS, of course, but 'IFRS as adopted by the European Union' (ARC, 2005; FEE, 2005). Nevertheless, the titles and the numbering of the standards have not been changed. No words have been changed and nothing has been added, and indeed that seems not to be allowed by the endorsement process.[9]

Having said that 'no words have been changed', we need again to refer to translation. The EU endorses many different language versions of the IASB's output.[10] Inevitably, this involves translation difficulties, including making errors (Evans, 2004; Nobes, 2006, p. 237). This is a further aspect of 'IFRS as adopted by the EU'.

Whether a company can simultaneously comply with EU-endorsed IFRS and IFRS as issued by the IASB is discussed later. However, this EU method of implementation is clearly different from 'adopting the process' as discussed in the previous section. The practical results include the different implementation dates and the different versions of IAS 39. Further, it would certainly be possible for major incompatibilities between the two sets of standards to open up, as seemed possible in October 2008 in the context of financial instruments (Zeff, 2010).

It is more difficult to categorise the position of South Africa for unlisted companies. For them, the IASB's standards and interpretations have had to be approved by the Accounting Practices Board (APB), whereby they are turned into South African GAAP. The Companies Act 2009 establishes a Financial Reporting Standards Council (to replace the APB) that approves the content of IFRS and recommend it to the appropriate government minister. The standards retain their IASB numbers and titles but are also given South African numbering.

This is a form of standard-by-standard endorsement. There might be scope in South Africa for deletions or other changes to IFRS. However, suppose that, in practice, no alterations are made, except that there would be a delay in making the IASB's output available. We could then put South African GAAP in the same category as South Africa (listed companies) above.

Fully converging?

Nobes (2008) suggested that the Australian method of implementing IFRS could be described as very close convergence. As Thomson (2009, p. 153) recorded, it involves the AASB in: changing the designation of the standards (e.g. from IAS 7 to AASB 107), adding references, inserting departures for not-for-profit entities and tabling the standards in the Australian Parliament. The AASB also adds a few disclosure requirements. The resulting standards are clearly different documents from the originals issued by the IASB. Thomson noted that the AASB referred to the package as 'Australian equivalents to IFRSs'.

One further aspect of the *initial* implementation of IFRS in Australia in 2005 was the deletion of a number of options from IFRS (e.g. the indirect method of calculating cash flows from IAS 7, and proportionate consolidation from IAS 31). Arguably, this improved the standards, but we suggest that it would be misleading to state that Australia had adopted IASs 7 and 31, and therefore that it had adopted IFRS in general. These deletions were reversed by the AASB in 2007. However, given these Australian precedents for differences from IFRS, there could in future be others, perhaps including incompatibilities with IFRS.

Removal by the AASB of the early-adoption options in IFRS was another feature that was confined to the initial implementation of IFRS. Since then, new Australian versions of IFRS leave any such options in place. The AASB has also been abandoning the term 'Australian equivalents to IFRSs' as it might be interpreted to imply less than full convergence with IFRS.

The current versions of the Australian standards (and even the initial ones of 2004) should ensure compliance with IFRS as issued by the IASB, as discussed below. However, the standards are not themselves 'as issued by the IASB'. We try to conclude, below, on an appropriate description for the Australian process.

Partially converging

Of course, there are examples of much less complete convergence than Australia has achieved. For instance, the Chinese adaptations of IFRS are very close in the case of some standards but not very close for others (e.g. impairment) (Deloitte, 2006). Despite this, the IASB's website showed China as one of the many countries that 'require or permit IFRSs', under the general heading of 'IFRS adoption and use around the world'.

Some other jurisdictions adopt IFRSs *en bloc* into national law, but not on a continuous basis. As a result, many new standards and amendments do not come into force when the IASB intended. The package of standards at any date might therefore be far from IFRS as issued by the IASB. This is the position, for example, for Venezuela.[11] That country is also shown, misleadingly, by the IASB's website as requiring or permitting IFRS.

So, what is adoption of IFRS?

We can now address the issue with which we began: was Thomson (2009) right to state that 'Australia definitely adopts IFRS'? Figure 7.1 portrays our characterisation of methods of implementing IFRS for the consolidated statements of listed companies in seven countries and the EU.[12] On the left is 'adopting the process', and that is clearly a method of 'adopting IFRS'. As we move further to the right in Figure 7.1, 'adoption' becomes less suitable as a description of the regulator's decision-making process. Let us suppose that Canada rapidly rubber-stamps all IFRS output and makes no translation errors into French. It would

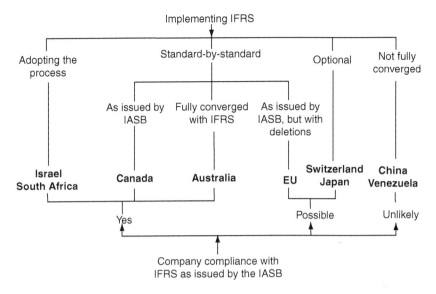

Figure 7.1 Methods of implementing IFRS (consolidated statements of listed companies).

then seem fair to say that it had adopted IFRS. Even so, to say that 'Israel and Canada have adopted IFRS' would be to obscure an important distinction.

By contrast, as noted earlier, Australia changes the designation of the standard, makes various textual changes, adds a few disclosure requirements, and (initially) removed early adoption and deleted options. Even now, there is a short delay between the issue of a standard by the IASB and its emergence from the Australian process. In our view, for these reasons, it is misleading to call this Australian implementation 'adoption of IFRS'. We, therefore, question Thomson's unadorned 'definitely adopts'. We admit that an appropriate term is hard to find. Above, we have a heading 'fully converging?'. Other possible descriptions are 'light screening' or 'standards that incorporate IFRS'. There is also a difficulty in describing the EU's version of IFRSs; perhaps they are 'as adapted' rather than 'as adopted'.

A related, but distinctly different, matter is whether entities in a jurisdiction comply with IFRS. To that we now turn.

Company compliance with IFRS

Irrespective of which of the above methods of implementation of IFRS is taken in a jurisdiction, there is still the question of whether a particular company complies or not with IFRS as issued by the IASB.

Even in jurisdictions that have adopted the IASB's process (e.g. Israel or South Africa), it would be possible for a company not to comply with IFRS if it inadvertently or deliberately broke the rules. By contrast, in the EU, companies are not required to comply with IFRS as issued by the IASB but can choose to do so, at the same time as fulfilling the legal requirement to follow IFRS as adopted by the EU. This is achieved by a company denying itself the extra opportunities for hedge accounting offered by the EU's version of IAS 39, i.e. with the carve-out. The other potential problem (the delay caused by endorsement) has so far not arisen, in the sense that all the IASB's output has been endorsed in time for its compulsory application.[13]

In Australia, at present, if companies comply with the Australian equivalents of IFRS, then they comply with IFRS as issued by the IASB. This was the case even when options (e.g. those in IASs 7 and 31) had been removed. However, under adaptations in other countries that are less close to the originals (e.g. the Chinese one), compliance with IFRS as issued by the IASB is unlikely to be achievable without producing non-statutory statements.

Of course, even if a jurisdiction has taken *none* of the above approaches to implementing IFRS, its companies might still be able to comply. For example, in Japan and Switzerland, IFRS is one of the possibilities in the requirements for the consolidated statements of listed companies. So, Japanese and Swiss groups can present statements that comply with IFRS as issued by the IASB for regulatory purposes. In 2012, this was common in Switzerland but not in Japan. The bottom part of Figure 7.1 records the position on company compliance for these countries and for the other jurisdictions mentioned above.

To what degree do auditors affirm compliance with IFRS as issued by the IASB in jurisdictions that have not 'adopted the process'? Nobes and Zeff (2008) examined the audit reports of companies included in the indices of the five largest stock exchanges of countries that had implemented IFRS in 2005/6: Australia, France, Germany, Spain and the UK.[14] They found that none of the French or Spanish audit reports affirmed compliance with IFRS as issued by the IASB, although 22 per cent of the German and 17 per cent of the British index companies did so. In the case of the British companies, this 'dual audit reporting' was generally achieved by presenting two separate audit opinions (one on EU-IFRS and one on IASB-IFRS). It was found most often for companies audited by one firm (Deloitte) and was associated with the company being SEC-registered.

Nobes and Zeff (2008, p. 281) suggest that most companies therefore do not grant to users (especially foreign users) one of the main benefits emerging from 40 years of international standardisation: helping the users to understand the financial reporting. That is, there is limited usefulness in a company complying with IFRS unless it asks the auditors to attest to that.

Most countries outside the EU have legislation or regulation which requires the auditor to affirm compliance with national GAAP, not with IFRS of any kind.

In 2005/6, the Australian position was of that type. That is, Australian companies were complying with IFRS as issued by the IASB but audit reports generally referred to compliance with Australian standards only. However, Australian (and New Zealand) *auditing* standards were changed in 2007 to require reference to both domestic standards and IFRS.[15]

7.3 Hypotheses relating to implementations of IFRS

Overview

This section explains three ways in which classification might still be helpful in the IFRS era. First, the degree to which national regulators allow or require IFRS for various purposes differs. This can be presented as a classification which could have been predicted by previous classifications. Second, the degree to which those individual national systems are converging with IFRS differs, in a way that classification can predict. Third, whether foreign countries' accounting systems are acceptable on particular exchanges, because they are IFRS or converging to IFRS, can be explained by classification.

Despite much criticism, discussed in Chapter 6, a two-group classification (Anglo versus continental European) is, in practice, frequently adopted in the literature (e.g. Guenther and Young, 2000; Hung, 2000; Ali and Hwang, 2000; Benston *et al.*, 2006, ch. 9; Ball *et al.*, 2000; La Porta *et al.*, 1997, 1998; Choi and Meek, 2005, pp. 56–59; Radebaugh *et al.*, 2006, pp. 55, 62; Walton *et al.*, 2003, pp. 6, 8). This section (based on Nobes, 2008) will specify a two-group classification including a large number of countries, and then see if it can be used for explanation and prediction.

I choose here to classify the member states of the European Union (EU) in 2006 plus two substantial countries outside the EU: Norway and Switzerland, which both have close ties with the EU. This 27-nation bloc is clearly defined economically and geographically, and there is useful accounting data on it, as will be seen below. I use my own previous writings to prepare the classification, so that readers can confirm that the classification has not been contrived *ex post* in order to prove the hypotheses raised. I apologise to readers for the amount of self-citation that this implies.

The Nobes (1983b) classification contains only nine of the above 27 European countries (shown with single asterisks in Table 7.1), partly because another eight of the countries had communist regimes at the time and therefore no 'financial reporting', and partly because some of the other countries are very small. However, Nobes (1992b, pp. 127–129) includes these nine plus a further five countries (shown with two asterisks in Table 7.1). The remaining 13 countries in the table are classified as follows. Slovenia and the three small Baltic states were not included in the above literature, but are classified like the other former communist states of the EU. Cyprus and Malta were again too small to be included. They are former British colonies and therefore classified on the left in accordance with Nobes (1998). Austria, Denmark, Finland, Greece, Luxembourg, Norway and Portugal are classified using various of the author's publications that comment on them (Nobes, 1992c, p. 3; Nobes, 1992d, p. 3; Nobes, 1992e, pp. 2–3; Nobes and Parker, 2004, p. 317; Nobes and Schwencke, 2006). IFRS is added, in accordance with Nobes (1998). It is intended that the objects being classified in Table 7.1 are not countries but accounting systems (i.e. the set of financial reporting practices) as under national laws and standards.

Table 7.1 A two-group accounting classification

Class A (strong equity, commercially driven)	Class B (weak equity, government driven, tax-dominated)
Ireland*	Belgium*
Netherlands*	France*
UK*	Germany*
Cyprus	Italy*
Denmark	Spain*
Malta	Sweden*
Norway	Czech Republic**
IFRS	Hungary**
	Poland**
	Slovakia**
	Switzerland**
	Austria
	Estonia
	Finland
	Greece
	Latvia
	Lithuania
	Luxembourg
	Portugal
	Slovenia

Notes
*=in Nobes (1983b).
**=added in Nobes (1992b).

National reactions to IFRS

Let us take the example of the 27 countries included in Table 7.1. For these, Table 7.2 shows whether or not companies are *required* to continue to use national accounting rules for unconsolidated accounting. Finland and Greece are excluded because different companies are treated differently: large companies with certain types of auditors are not required to use national rules, although the bulk of companies are.

The simple classification of Table 7.2 illustrates the 'sharpens description' use of a classification. It tells a story simply and clearly. However, as usual, the truth is more complicated than can easily be captured in a classification, as the notes to Table 7.2 explain. For example, some larger German companies are allowed to publish IFRS unconsolidated statements but only if they also prepare statements under national rules for the purposes of the calculation of taxable and distributable profits (Haller and Eierle, 2004).

Would previous accounting classifications have enabled a prediction of Table 7.2, and do they help to explain it? A prediction from the literature would be that countries in the right-hand column of Table 7.1 would not allow IFRS for unconsolidated accounting, as now explained. First, the use of IFRS would change profit figures, so in countries where tax and accounting are closely linked, the

Table 7.2 Whether European countries mandate national rules for unconsolidated accounting

Not required	Required
Cyprus	Austria
Denmark	Belgium
Estonia	Czech Republic[1]
Ireland	France
Italy	Germany[2]
Luxembourg	Hungary
Malta	Latvia
Netherlands	Lithuania
Norway	Poland[1]
Slovenia	Portugal
UK	Slovakia[3]
	Spain
	Sweden
	Switzerland

Source: prepared by author from http://ec.europa.eu/internal_market/accounting/docs/ias/ias-use-of-options_en.pdf (accessed 5 May 2007).

Notes
1 Except for listed companies.
2 Required for tax and distribution accounting but, for large companies, not for publication.
3 Except for 'public interest' companies.

rules for the calculation of taxable income would in effect be put into the hands of the IASB, which is specifically uninterested in tax (IASB *Framework*, para. 6). This would obviously be politically and economically unacceptable. In principle, tax and financial reporting could be de-coupled in such countries but that would be a major philosophical and practical problem. The same reasoning applies to the calculation of prudently distributable income, which again rests directly on accounting numbers in, for example, Germany but is de-coupled in various ways in the UK.[16] So, Germany could not easily allow the use of IFRS for the calculation of distributable income. Another issue is that, in some right-hand-column countries, some of the requirements of IFRS are seen as unsatisfactory for legal reasons related to unconsolidated reporting. For example, in France, the capitalisation of finance leases as required by IFRS is regarded as showing fictitious assets on an entity's balance sheet, thus misleading creditors (e.g. Standish, 2000, p. 200).

Would the classification of Table 7.1 have successfully predicted Table 7.2? The relevant hypothesis can be stated as:

H1 A country with a national accounting system on the right in Table 7.1 will not allow IFRS for unconsolidated accounting (i.e. the country will also be on the right in Table 7.2).

The null hypothesis is:

> H01 The classification of countries in Table 7.2 is only associated by chance with the classification in Table 7.1.

A chi-square test enables one to reject the null hypothesis at more than 99 per cent significance. So, H1 can be accepted. Indeed, the only countries that are not correctly classified by using Table 7.1 are Estonia, Italy and Luxembourg. Estonia has presumably taken the view that it wishes to move as fast as possible from its communist past to modern, international practice. Luxembourg has a long history of extending to companies any choices that are available within EU rules (Clark, 1994, p. 107). One explanation for Italy granting permission to use IFRS is that Italy also likes to be seen to be modern and international and that, in practice, companies will not volunteer to use IFRS for their unconsolidated statements because they would then have to produce a different set for tax purposes. Nevertheless, in principle, tax and financial reporting can now be separate in Italy, which is a major change to law.[17]

The analysis of this section can be extended to other countries. For example, because Australia, New Zealand and South Africa would be on the left of Table 7.1 (e.g. see Nobes, 1992b, p. 127), they would be on the left of Table 7.2. In China, by contrast, which would have been put on the right of Table 7.1 (see Nobes, 1998), IFRS was only used in 2006 in the consolidated statements of some listed companies.[18]

Continuing national rules

The previous subsection explains that, in many countries, IFRS is not allowed for unconsolidated accounting. Consequently, in Europe, IFRS is concentrated on the consolidated statements of listed companies. There are about 8,000 listed companies amongst the millions of companies in Europe. Therefore, the great bulk of accounting in Europe and in other continents (e.g. South America) continues under national accounting systems.

For multinational groups, for international audit firms and for tax authorities dealing with such entities, an appropriate classification of the accounting systems can remain a preliminary part of understanding the international differences. For example, Table 7.1 coupled with a list of typical accounting features to be found in the two groups (e.g. as in Table 3.5) would be a start for understanding European accounting differences.

Different degrees of convergence with IFRS

Given that national accounting systems have survived in many jurisdictions, at least for some purposes, a further issue is their convergence with IFRS. This process is the main explanation of change in accounting rules since 2000. The word 'convergence' is accurate when applied to the joint programme of the IASB and the US's Financial Accounting Standards Board (FASB) because both have changed particular standards towards each other's[19] and have run many joint projects (e.g. on performance reporting, deferred tax and revenue recognition). However, in the case of other countries, 'convergence with IFRS' is a euphemism for piecemeal adoption of IFRS.

The degree to which a jurisdiction's national accounting system is being changed towards IFRS varies. For example, in the UK, eight accounting standards (FRSs 20 to 26 and 29) were copies of international standards. By contrast, German rules related to unconsolidated statements (the *Handelsgesetzbuch*) did not change at all until some minor changes in 2009.[20]

An hypothesis for explaining this difference between countries is similar to the first hypothesis, relating to national reactions to IFRS. That is, some aspects of IFRS can be regarded as imprudent for the calculation of distributable income and for the protection of creditors. Other aspects can be regarded as unsuitable for a tax base, e.g. greater use of fair values or of estimations (such as IAS 11's percentage-of-completion method for contract accounting). Therefore, it is proposed:

H2 A country with a national accounting system on the right of Table 7.1 will be slower (than those on the left) to converge with IFRS.

It is more difficult, than for H1, to measure this with precision. However, examples are easy to find, as in the convergence comparison of Germany and the UK above. Other systems on the left (e.g. Cyprus, Malta; and Australia) have been abandoned or converged out of existence. By contrast, there is no detectable movement in Belgium. This time, even Italy fits the hypothesis. It is on the right of Table 7.1, and its national system for unconsolidated statements has changed little since 2000.[21] It seems likely that the hypothesis could be confirmed by further research.

Acceptable accounting by foreign issuers

At the time of writing, the SEC accepts only US GAAP reporting from its US registrants. It accepts IFRS from foreign registrants, requiring any other reporting to be reconciled to US GAAP. However, EU exchanges accepted reporting in a number of GAAPs, under certain conditions related to their convergence with IFRS (CESR, 2007). From 2009, only IFRS or accounting 'equivalent to IFRS' are accepted.

The former Committee of European Securities Regulators (CESR) analysed whether the GAAPs used by over 90 per cent of the issuers on European exchanges satisfy the pre-2009 conditions for acceptance by those exchanges.

Table 7.3 summarises its conclusions, which are a combination of two issues: (i) the non-EU countries that are home jurisdictions for EU listers, and (ii) whether the GAAP of those countries is converged or converging with IFRS or similar. Could the content of Table 7.3 have been predicted and can it be explained? The hypothesis would be that foreign listed companies tend to come from 'strong equity' countries (in terms of Table 7.1), and that such countries would have accounting similar to IFRS or have adopted IFRS. So:

> H3 Foreign countries whose companies list on EU exchanges and whose GAAP is, according to CESR, acceptably close to IFRS are Class A countries.

Inspection of Table 7.3 reveals that, of the 12 jurisdictions in its top two categories of clear acceptance, 11 are present or former dependencies of the UK and one of the Netherlands. According to Nobes (1998), all these countries would therefore be classified on the left of Table 7.1. We do not in this case need statistics to accept Hypothesis H3, as there are no exceptions.

7.4 Classification by IFRS practices

Introduction

Chapter 6 examined the large number of intrinsic accounting classifications made in the pre-IFRS era. It was noted there that none of the classifications were based on the observation of actual practices in annual reports. This section

Table 7.3 Home jurisdictions of EU foreign issuers

Issuers from these countries should be able to include in the notes to the financial statements a statement of compliance with IFRS, as these countries have adopted IFRS.	• Australia • Hong Kong • New Zealand • South Africa • Singapore
These countries do not have 'national GAAP' as such and their issuers apparently apply US GAAP, IFRS or Canadian GAAP.	• Cayman Islands • Bermuda • Netherlands Antilles • Isle of Man • Jersey • Guernsey • British Virgin Islands
The countries on the right could qualify … as CESR found that there is a public statement of a convergence programme.	• Taiwan • China • Brazil

Source: adapted by the author from CESR (2007, p. 2).

studies an intrinsic classification made by Nobes (2011) which is different in two major respects: it classifies countries by their IFRS practices, and it actually collects data on those practices.

As will be seen, the objects classified are eight countries or, rather, the IFRS practices in the consolidated statements of large listed companies in those countries.

For the countries examined, the rules are identical,[22] so there is complete *de jure* harmony; no differences would be measured if rules were being assessed and no classification would be possible. However, there are large international differences in IFRS practices (as explained in Section 3.8), and interesting classification results.

Countries included

One sustained debate in the area concerns whether the two-group classification (Anglo versus continental European) can be substantiated. Cairns (1997), Alexander and Archer (2000) and d'Arcy (2001) dispute the dichotomy, whereas Mueller (1967), Nobes (1983b) and Doupnik and Salter (1993) support it. A summary of reasons suggested for why those who dispute the two-group classification fail to find it is as follows: they concentrate on non-representative accounting (i.e. on the consolidated statements of a few large companies in continental Europe),[23] or they concentrate on the regulatory system rather than on accounting practices,[24] or they use erroneous data (as discussed in Chapter 6).

Despite the doubts of some of the theorists, much empirical literature on other accounting topics includes a two-group classification as an independent variable, in many cases based on the related common law/code law split (e.g. Guenther and Young, 2000; Hung, 2000; Ali and Hwang, 2000; Ball *et al.*, 2000; Hope, 2003; Barniv *et al.*, 2005).

A note on the Netherlands is needed because it has created problems for the classifiers examined in Chapter 6. Da Costa *et al.* (1978) find that the Netherlands is unusual and cannot be classified. Frank (1979) puts the Netherlands in a US group, but Nair and Frank (1980) using a subset of the same data put the Netherlands in a UK group. Figure 6.1 of the previous chapter (which is from Nobes, 1983b) shows the Netherlands as an outlier of the Anglo group. Parker (1991, p. 229) describes Dutch accounting as '*sui generis*'. D'Arcy (2001), using more recent data, shows the Netherlands in a continental group but outside its core. It is therefore difficult to create a clear hypothesis concerning the position of the Netherlands. The country is usually included with continental Europe in the empirical studies mentioned above.

This section investigates whether the old two-group classification (as in Figure 6.1) persists even in the recent IFRS practices of large listed companies. If there is scope for pre-IFRS practice to affect choices of IFRS policies (Nobes, 2006; Kvaal and Nobes, 2010) and if EU harmonisation of accounting had worked well, then one might no longer expect to see EU countries on different sides of a two-group classification of the IFRS practices. In particular, one might expect the UK to be grouped with other EU countries rather than with Australia. However, given the discussion at the start of this section about continuing reasons for international differences, Nobes (2011) hypothesises that the two-group classification of Figure 6.1 will still be found in the 2008/9 accounting policy choices made by companies using IFRS.

The method of choosing the countries for investigation here begins with the 14 countries of Figure 6.1. Kvaal and Nobes (2010) investigated the IFRS practices of companies in the five IFRS-using countries with the largest stock markets. All of these are in Figure 6.1. Of the other countries in that figure, the lack of IFRS data means that I cannot yet add Canada, Japan and the USA for this study. I propose to add the next three largest IFRS-using capital markets of Figure 6.1, i.e. Italy, the Netherlands and Sweden.[25] By doing this, I ensure that all seven of the 'families' of Figure 6.1 are represented. The only IFRS-using countries of Figure 6.1 that are excluded from this study are Belgium, Ireland and New Zealand, which have few listed companies of the same size as those examined here for the other countries.[26]

This study, then, includes eight countries. Of these, seven (i.e. all but Australia) are in the European Union (including the largest four of the original six EU members, plus the UK which joined in 1973, Spain which joined in 1986 and Sweden which joined in 1995). All seven had implemented the main EU accounting harmonisation measures (the Fourth and Seventh Directives on company law) by 1995.[27]

The use of the largest companies and of 2008/9 data should provide the strongest test for the hypothesis, for the following reasons. The expectation is that the largest companies are the most likely to be affected by international influences and therefore the least likely to conform to national traditions. Also, Kvaal and Nobes (2012) show that the influence of nationality on IFRS practices had slightly decreased from 2005/6 (mostly a transition year) to 2008/9. So, if there is a two-group classification for the largest companies in 2008/9, one can have confidence that it would be found for the generality of companies and for 2005/6.

Data

Kvaal and Nobes (2010; hereafter K&N) studied company choices on all 16 of the IFRS policy options for which they concluded that the choice was observable. This included nine presentation topics and seven measurement topics. K&N note that some topics are more important than others, but that they all contribute towards answering the question whether pre-IFRS national practices continue under IFRS and whether IFRS practice on any topic is significantly different across countries. K&N do not add the topics together, so weighting is not an issue.

By contrast, for classification, the issue of weighting is important. It is discussed by Nobes (1981) and by d'Arcy (2004), and is returned to at length in Chapter 8. It can be argued that measurement topics are more important than presentation topics. It is proposed here to delete three presentation topics from

K&N's list: (i) whether a balance sheet shows an increasing or a decreasing liquidity order, (ii) whether an income statement includes a line for 'operating profit' and (iii) the position of dividends received in a cash flow statement. The remaining 13 policy topics are shown in Table 7.4; the first six relating to presentation, and the next seven to measurement. However, I check for robustness by adding back some of these topics, as explained later.

The issue of weighting still remains. All the classification studies use equal weightings because of the difficulty of justifying any other approach. Nevertheless, inspection of the data used in previous papers, reveals that some topics are much less important than others.[28] Here, an attempt has been made to exclude the least important topics, so equal weighting is more defensible.

As explained in Chapter 6, Nair and Frank (1980) usefully separate measurement practices from disclosure practices. This is more problematic here for the

Table 7.4 IFRS policy options

1*	(a)	balance sheet shows assets = credits
	(b)	focusing on net assets
2*	(a)	income statement by function
	(b)	by nature
3*	(a)	equity accounting profit in 'operating'
	(b)	below
4	(a)	Statement of Changes in Equity
	(b)	SORIE/OCI, excluding owner transactions
5*	(a)	direct operating cash flows
	(b)	indirect
6*	(a)	interest paid as operating cash flow
	(b)	as financing
7	(a)	only cost for PPE
	(b)	some fair value
8	(a)	investment property at cost
	(b)	at fair value
9*	(a)	some financial assets designated at fair value
	(b)	not
10	(a)	capitalisation of interest on construction
	(b)	expensing
11*	(a)	FIFO for inventory cost
	(b)	weighted average
12	(a)	actuarial gains/losses to SORIE/OCI
	(b)	corridor method, or to income in full
13	(a)	proportional consolidation of joint ventures
	(b)	equity method

Note
*=non-financial companies only.

statistical methods because it reduces the number of topics in each of the two categories to fewer than regarded as suitable for separate tests. However, I investigate the results of separating measurement from disclosure under 'Robustness' below.

For the five countries studied by K&N, I use the data of Kvaal and Nobes (2012) from the 2008/9 financial statements of the largest listed companies. For the additional three countries, I again choose the largest listed companies by taking all the companies in the *Financial Times* 'Europe 500' at 31 March 2009. This means 29 Italian companies, 17 Dutch and 26 Swedish. Two Italian companies are then deleted because one used US GAAP and another was a subsidiary. For the remaining total of 70 companies from the three countries, I hand pick data on the IFRS options from the financial reports[29] for the year ended 31 December 2008 or nearest after.

In all, the sample is 287 IFRS financial statements. Table 7.5 shows the composition of the sample companies by country and sector. Jaafar and McLeay (2007) warn of a related problem that researchers into classification or harmonisation have not adjusted for, or even mentioned. That is, some apparent lack of harmony in accounting practices (within or between countries) may be justifiable because it is caused by differences in underlying economic transactions and therefore the different accounting practices might not hamper comparability. Jaafar and McLeay (p. 158) give the example of inventory accounting, where the choice of FIFO or LIFO might be related to particular real usage of inventory, and that might vary by sector of the economy. On investigation of this and two other accounting topics (depreciation method and goodwill treatment), they find some small effect of sector, but it is greatly outweighed by the effect of country.

None of the classifications in Chapters 5 and 6 mentions this sector issue. I present the sectoral mix of the sample for inspection by readers. Some of the companies are in financial sectors. I follow K&N by including such companies but only for certain policy topics. For example, I exclude financial companies

Table 7.5 Country and sector* distribution

	Australia	UK	Germany	France	Spain	NL	Italy	Sweden
0 Oil and gas	3	4	0	1	1	1	2	0
1 Basic materials	5	10	3	1	2	0	0	3
2 Industrials	5	3	5	7	7	5	5	6
3 Consumer goods	1	9	6	7	0	4	0	5
4 Health care	2	5	1	2	0	0	0	1
5 Consumer services	6	22	4	6	4	2	1	1
6 Telecommunications	1	3	1	1	1	1	1	2
7 Utilities	1	7	2	3	5	0	5	0
8 Financials	16	21	7	4	7	3	13	7
9 Technology	0	1	1	2	1	1	0	1
Total	40	85	30	34	28	17	27	26

Note
* Sectors according to Industry Classification Benchmark.

from the data on cash flow statements because these companies have different rules from others. Table 7.4 shows which topics are excluded for financial companies. In Chapter 8, the potential effect of including/excluding sectors is investigated further.

Methodology

Frank (1979) and Nair and Frank (1980) use principal component analysis (factor analysis) in order to reveal groupings of countries that have similar accounting according to a database of accounting rules and practices. The results were checked by using multidimensional scaling. D'Arcy (2001) uses a different database and applies cluster analysis and produces dendrograms. She also uses multidimensional scaling. These methods were outlined in Section 6.1.

All three of the above approaches are used in this section. The expectation is that they will all lead to similar results, although presented in different graphical ways. However, if clear differences between the results of the different methods were to emerge, that would be a warning of problems in the data.

Results

IFRS choices

Table 7.6 shows, by country, the percentages of companies that chose particular IFRS options. Inspection reveals wide variation among the countries. Long-running traditions[30] continue, such as: (i) the use of a by-nature income statement in Italy and Spain (topic 2), (ii) the willingness to depart from historical cost in the Netherlands (topics 7, 8 and 9), (iii) the use of the weighted average method for inventory costing in Germany, Italy and Spain (topic 11) and (iv) the use of proportional consolidation in France and Spain (topic 13). As explained earlier, K&N show, for five of the countries, that the differences between these national patterns are highly statistically significant.

For most of the 13 topics, data is available for all companies studied. However, there is very limited data for some countries on one topic:[31] the measurement of investment properties (topic 8 in Tables 7.4 and 7.6). Therefore, for some purposes below, I report on results using only the remaining 12 topics. I discuss the issue further below under 'Robustness'.

Principal component analysis

As explained in Section 6.1, principal component analysis (sometimes called 'factor analysis') processes the data in order to look for 'components' that are selections of practices with different weights that best explain the variance between the objects of study (in this case, countries). In this case, three such components were identified, explaining 85 per cent of the variance.[32] As an example, component 2 (on which Australia and the UK load highly) contains

Table 7.6 Policy choices (percentages of companies by country), 2008/9

		Australia	UK	Germany	France	Spain	NL	Italy	Sweden
1 (b)	focusing on net assets	100.0	85.2	0.0	0.0	0.0	14.3	0.0	0.0
2 (a)	income statement by function	58.3	82.1	82.6	62.1	4.8	50.0	7.1	95.0
3 (a)	equity profit in 'operating'	68.8	42.6	22.7	10.0	0.0	0.0	0.0	93.3
4 (b)	SORIE/OCI only	67.5	90.6	36.7	14.7	32.1	41.1	18.8	23.1
5 (b)	indirect cash flows	8.3	100.0	100.0	100.0	87.5	100.0	100.0	100.0
6 (a)	interest paid as 'operating' flow	81.5	65.1	68.2	80.0	47.6	78.5	92.9	90.0
7 (b)	some PPE at fair value	15.0	11.1	0.0	0.0	0.0	11.8	0.0	3.8
8 (b)	investment property at fair value	39.3	70.8	5.3	14.3	13.3	75.0	5.6	100.0
9 (a)	some fair value designation	25.0	11.1	17.4	33.3	19.0	75.0	12.5	52.6
10 (a)	interest capitalisation	84.4	57.7	41.7	44.4	100.0	66.6	27.8	33.3
11 (b)	weighted average only	52.9	30.0	75.0	50.0	88.2	41.7	78.6	10.0
12 (a)	actuarial gains/losses to SORIE	86.7	86.4	63.3	50.0	63.2	31.3	20.8	20.0
13 (a)	proportional consolidation	11.5	23.3	15.8	75.8	91.3	46.0	39.1	33.3

several of the choices of Table 7.4: a focus on net assets, the use of the SORIE/OCI (including for actuarial gains and losses),[33] the use of fair value and the lack of use of proportional consolidation.

Then, each country is assigned to the component on which it loads the greatest.[34] Table 7.7 shows the component scores for the countries (using 12 topics).[35] As may be seen, there are two groups: 'continental' countries exhibit component 1, 'Anglo' countries component 2, with Sweden as an outlier. The UK is nearer to the continental group than is Australia. Germany is the nearest continental country to the Anglo group.

Sampling adequacy is checked by a Kaiser-Meyer-Olkin measure which can take values of 0 to 1. In this case, the score is 0.74, which is fairly good (Hutcheson and Sofroniou, 1999).

Cluster analysis

Nobes (1983b) and d'Arcy (2001) use cluster analysis. Following d'Arcy, I use the method of average linkage between groups. The process first identifies the congruence in policies between each pair of countries. It identifies the most similar pair, in this case Germany and France. It then fuses these two together as a single unit and looks for the next nearest pairing, and so on. The result is shown as Figure 7.2.[36] The vertical branching lines rise as each new country is added, showing increasing dissimilarity. In this case, Italy, the Netherlands and Spain are gradually added to Germany and France. Meanwhile, Australia and the UK form their own pair. Lastly, Sweden joins the fused continental group.

Multidimensional scaling

Both Frank (1979) and d'Arcy (2001) check their results with multidimensional scaling. Figure 7.3 shows the result for the 'modern' non-metrical solution using two dimensions (Gordon, 1981, ch. 5). Again the two-group classification is clear, with Germany and the Netherlands nearer than other continentals to the

Table 7.7 Component scores by country (12 topics)

Country	Component		
	1	*2*	*3*
Australia	−0.0997	0.6978	−0.1803
Sweden	0.0075	−0.0294	0.7814
UK	0.0860	0.6599	0.1605
Germany	0.3452	0.2548	0.2416
France	0.4405	−0.0551	0.1708
Spain	0.5354	−0.0122	−0.4620
Netherlands	0.3951	−0.0908	0.1705
Italy	0.4760	−0.0173	−0.0342

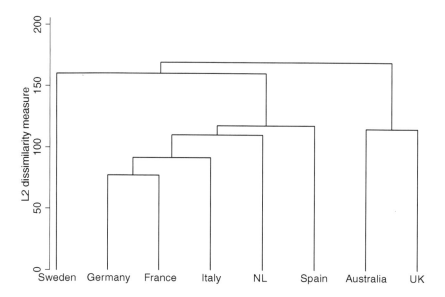

Figure 7.2 Dendrogram of two-cluster solution.

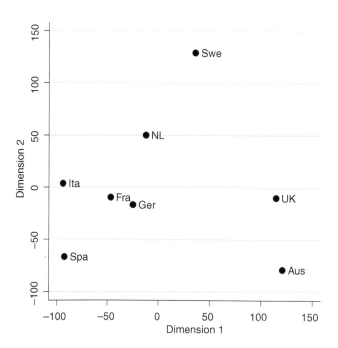

Figure 7.3 Multidimensional scaling of two dimensions.

Anglo group. Very similar pictures result from the 'classical' metric solution. According to the Mardia measure of goodness of fit, 93.0 per cent of the variation is explained by the two dimensions.[37]

Robustness

The above three classification methods were run again after adding back the presentation issues relating to the income statement and balance sheet that had been excluded on grounds of limited importance (see previous section). The basic conclusions were the same.

I also tried three further robustness checks. As reported above, topic 8 was eliminated because there was little data on it for some countries. This had little effect; various footnotes record the small differences in statistics for 12 topics as opposed to 13 topics. Second, I ran the models using only the seven 'measurement' topics of Table 7.4. Here, again, the results show Australia and the UK together. This time, the Netherlands and Sweden are also shown together, driven partly by their high scores for the use of fair value on topic 8 which rests on data from very few companies. I also tried running all the models without Sweden, which shows some outlier features. This did not alter the classification of the remaining seven countries.

Synthesis

The three statistical techniques come to the same conclusion, which is that the IFRS practices of very large companies show a two-group classification: Anglo and continental European. The Netherlands is not in the Anglo group, although its practices do stand out on certain issues. Dutch, German and Swedish practices are the nearest continental ones to the Anglo group. Australian practices are furthest from the continental group. It was anticipated that three similar pictures would result, and this allows some confidence in the conclusion.

7.5 Conclusions

Using somewhat informal data,[38] based largely on impressions of practices of companies in 1980, Nobes (1983b) proposed a classification of the accounting systems of 14 countries (discussed in Chapter 6 and shown there as Figure 6.1). The first split of countries was into two groups, with Australia and the UK in one group and most continental European countries in the other. That classification was drawn up before any of the EU's Directives on accounting had been implemented and before any company in any of the countries considered here had adopted IFRS.

I ask here whether it is possible to discern the same classification after 30 years of harmonisation efforts by the EU and the IASC/B. Of the 14 countries of Figure 6.1, I remove the three not yet using IFRS, then take those with the eight largest capital markets; meaning that only three small IFRS-using countries are excluded. I then put hand-pick data on 2008/9 IFRS policy choices into a series of statistical classification techniques.

The data used here relate to accounting itself rather than to influences on accounting (e.g. as in Mueller, 1967, 1968) or to regulatory systems (e.g. as in Alexander and Archer, 2000). Further, the data measure accounting *practices* rather than accounting rules (as in d'Arcy, 2001) or a mixture of rules and opinions on practices (as in da Costa *et al.*, 1978; Frank, 1979; Nair and Frank, 1980). This is the first classification to be based on practices, and the first in the context of IFRS. In this case, it is very clear that the use of practices is more relevant than the use of rules, because all eight countries were using the same rules.

All the statistical techniques lead to the same conclusion: Anglo and continental European groupings can be discerned in the IFRS practices of very large companies. I explain earlier why this is likely to be the case, a fortiori, in earlier periods or for smaller companies. The Netherlands is shown here in the continental group (though not centrally), and it had always been difficult to classify. As in the 1980 classification of Figure 6.1, Sweden is in the continental group, but noticeably different from the rest.

Some limitations of this study are that I look at only the largest listed companies and only for the latest year available when the data was collected. However, as explained, I believe that this represents the toughest test. Other researchers could extend the study and add more countries. Second, there might be some effect of sector rather than country, given that the sectoral mix is not exactly the same for each country. However, research suggests that this is likely to be small; an issue to be investigated further in Chapter 8. I also admit that equal weighting of topics is arbitrary, although I have eliminated cosmetic topics.

I do not suggest that there has been no harmonisation in 30 years. On some major topics, IFRS practice is more standardised than previous international practices were, e.g. LIFO has been banned, all subsidiaries are consolidated and finance leases are capitalised. However, for many topics, national patterns have continued into IFRS practice, and groupings of countries are still in place. As mentioned, I have excluded data on several cosmetic issues that also show these patterns and groupings. I believe that the patterns would also exist for important topics that cannot easily be measured, such as the tendency to recognise impairments or to capitalise development costs. It might be possible for other researchers to gather data on these.

I conclude that the findings add to the evidence that accounting practices flow from deep-seated and long-lasting national influences, so that the practices are resistant even to sustained attempts at international harmonisation. If the EU's harmonisation efforts had succeeded, one would not expect to see the UK still classified with Australia rather than with the other EU countries. This confirms the EU's wisdom in abandoning its harmonisation efforts, when it comes to listed companies' consolidated statements, in favour of IFRS. The overall objective of the IASB is to increase comparability of financial reporting.[39] This is at its most relevant for the large listed companies, examined in this chapter, that are all using IFRS. However, even for them, the chapter shows that there are clear country-related differences that would hamper comparability. The IASB's objective includes narrowing differences in practice by changing the regulations. For most of the topics studied here,[40] there is no obvious justification, in terms of underlying economic differences, for the variations in practice that result from the choices allowed. The implication is that the continued availability of these choices conflicts with the IASB's objectives.

Notes

1 The standard is entitled 'Adopting International Financial Reporting Standards'. Paragraph 3 requires entities subject to the Securities Law to use IFRS for periods starting on or after 1 January 2008.
2 Even without 'errors', translation of accounting terms is fraught with difficulty (Evans, 2004).
3 We are grateful for advice here from Marion Kirsh, Associate Chief Accountant of the Ontario Securities Commission and from Tricia O'Malley, Chair of Canada's Accounting Standards Board.
4 Some translations are 'official' in that they are reviewed by a committee of the IASC Foundation. CICA will be the official translator into Canadian French.
5 European Parliament legislative resolution of 14 November 2007 on COM (2006) 0918-C6-0029/2007-2006/0298 (COD).
6 Even the mandatory date can be different. For example, IFRIC 12 was endorsed by the EU in March 2009 containing a mandatory adoption date later than that as issued by the IASB.
7 For example, it is informally accepted in the EU (e.g. Accounting Regulatory Committee meeting of 2 February 2007) that a parent company that is exempted under a national law from preparing consolidated statements is exempted under EU-IFRS even if not by IAS 27.
8 See, for example, the 'EU endorsement status report' at efrag.org.
9 That is, the Commission and others can endorse or not. In the crisis surrounding the initial endorsement of IAS 39, this was interpreted as allowing deletions but not amendments.
10 In 2010, there are 22 versions.
11 The Deloitte website (iasplus.com, accessed 17 February 2010) states that Venezuela has not adopted any new IASB documents since 2004.
12 In some cases, the implementation spreads further (e.g. to unlisted entities or to unconsolidated statements) but the story then becomes very complex.
13 An example of last-minute endorsement was that of IAS 1 as amended by the IASB in September 2007, to be in force for periods beginning on or after 1 January 2009. This was endorsed by the EU on 18 December 2008. As mentioned in footnote 5, IFRIC 12 (required for 31 December 2008 statements) was not endorsed until 29 March 2009, but could have been complied with because it was not inconsistent with endorsed-IFRS.
14 For example, the indices used were the ASX 50, CAC 40, DAX 30, IBEX 35 and FTSE 100.
15 ASA 700 of the Australian Auditing and Assurance Standards Board.
16 For example, extra depreciation caused by revaluing assets is not deemed to affect distributable income. This and many other issues are, in effect, controlled by the accountancy bodies (e.g. ICAEW 2004).
17 Legislative Decree of 28 February 2005, no. 38.
18 For 2007, new standards (ASBEs), based closely on IFRS, are in force for Chinese listed companies, and available for others.

19 Convergence is the main explanation for the issuance of IFRS 5, IFRS 8 and IAS 23 (as revised in 2007); and of SFASs 150, 153, 154, 159.

20 Confirmation by Cornelia Flury of the *Institut der Wirtschaftsprüfer*, 26 June 2007.

21 Confirmation by Johannes Guigard, PricewaterhouseCoopers, Milan, 26 June 2007.

22 None of the countries uses 'IFRS as issued by the IASB' (see Section 7.2). However, any differences caused by that do not affect the topics studied in this section.

23 Cairns (1997) illustrates his argument by reference to a few large German companies, which were certainly moving away from traditional German practices by the middle of the 1990s. However, this only related to those few companies and only to their consolidated statements.

24 Nobes (2003) suggests that this is the case in Alexander and Archer (2000).

25 By market capitalisation; see World Federation of Stock Exchanges at www.world-exchanges.org/statistics.

26 There are only 12 Belgian companies and two Irish companies of matching size (see the section on 'Data and methodology' below). The New Zealand exchange had less than half the market capitalisation of the Irish one.

27 Spain implemented with a law of 1989, Italy in 1991 and Sweden in 1995.

28 Nobes (1981) investigates this in detail.

29 For all eight countries, all the reports were available in English, and those reports were used. For a related project on smaller listed companies, a sample of French and Spanish reports was examined in both English and original forms. No differences of substance were detected. This allows some confidence that the data collected had not been affected by translation issues.

30 These are reported in many books on national accounting practices, such as Alexander and Archer (2003), which has country chapters on all the European countries studied here.

31 For example, only three Swedish and four Dutch companies disclosed an accounting policy on this issue.

32 This is for 12 topics; it was 84 per cent for 13 topics.

33 That is, the presentation of a main financial statement to show other comprehensive income (OCI). In 2008/9 this was called a Statement of Recognised Income and Expense (SORIE).

34 After varimax rotation.

35 That is, excluding the measurement of investment property because of thin data, as explained above.

36 For the 13-topic solution. A similar picture emerges for the 12-topic solution.

37 For the classical solution with 13 topics; 93.9 per cent for 12 topics.

38 The measures in Nobes (1983b) were not based directly on a formal sample of company practices but on rules and on general observations of practices in the countries concerned.

39 Paragraph 2 of the *Constitution* of 2010, and in the *Introduction* to the *Framework* as revised in 2010.

40 Financial companies might need special rules on some issues (e.g. cash flow statements) for which they have been omitted from the data here. Inventory valuation and the valuation of investment properties might be areas where differences (though perhaps not choices) could be justified by sector or by type of transaction.

8   Are the classifications merely arbitrary?

8.1 A meta-analysis

In this section, I provide a meta-analysis of all the classifications of accounting systems. Then Section 8.2 summarises the lessons about accounting classification from Chapters 4 to 7. Then, in the rest of the chapter, I ask whether any of the classifications can be seen as reliable. Of course, some are decades old, so must be judged by whether they were reliable at the time and must be treated with especial caution for any current use. In later sections, an experiment is performed to see how sensitive classifications are to changes in such issues as the countries and sectors included and the characteristics used to measure the countries (or systems).

Meta-analysis is a procedure which mathematically integrates the results of previous independent studies. It can reduce the importance of unbiased errors in the data or the procedures of particular individual studies. Meta-analysis is frequently used in medical research, in which context Egger *et al.* (1997) note that attention must be paid to the selection and weighting of previous studies. For our meta-analysis of accounting classifications,[1] we include all the studies of Table 4.1 with equal weights, in the absence of any objective alternative. Our analysis covers the 15 countries which host the world's largest economies and which have been included in previous classifications. The countries included are those for which we collect IFRS data for our experiments below (except China), plus the largest remaining countries: Brazil, India, Japan and the United States. Russia is excluded because it was only found in two previous classifications, and not in terms of published financial reporting. China is excluded because it was not in any of the former classifications. As will be explained in the next paragraph, ours is not a traditional meta-analysis which combines studies by significance levels (see e.g. Christie, 1990), because the results of classification studies are the groupings of countries and not significance levels.

Table 8.1 shows the meta-analysis: the bottom-left triangle relates to all the classifications, the top-right triangle to the intrinsic ones only. For each pair of countries, the figure shown is the percentage of the classifications which placed that pair in the same group. The bracketed number shows how many classifications included the pair. For example, the bottom-left pairing of Japan and the US

Table 8.1 Meta-analysis of classifications: percentages with which pairs of countries are grouped together (% (N))

	US	AU	UK	CA	HK	FR	ES	IT	DE	CH	ZA	SK	BR	IN	JP
US	–	29 (7)	22 (9)	83 (6)	50 (2)	13* (8)	14 (7)	17 (6)	25 (8)	20 (5)	20 (5)	50 (2)	20 (5)	25 (4)	43 (7)
AU	40 (10)	–	75 (8)	33 (6)	50 (2)	0* (8)	0* (8)	0* (8)	0* (8)	0* (5)	80 (5)	0 (2)	20 (5)	25 (4)	14 (7)
UK	33 (15)	82* (11)	–	50 (6)	100 (2)	22 (9)	0* (8)	0* (7)	11* (9)	20 (5)	100* (5)	0 (2)	0* (5)	0* (4)	0* (7)
CA	88* (8)	50 (8)	63 (8)	–	100* (4)	17 (6)	0* (6)	0* (5)	17 (6)	0* (4)	50 (4)	0 (2)	0* (4)	0 (3)	33 (6)
HK	75 (4)	75 (4)	100* (4)	100* (4)	–	50 (2)	0 (2)	0 (2)	0 (2)	0 (1)	100 (2)	0 (2)	0 (2)	0 (1)	0 (2)
FR	8* (13)	0* (11)	14* (14)	13* (8)	25 (4)	–	63 (8)	71 (7)	78 (9)	80 (5)	20 (5)	50 (2)	40 (5)	25 (4)	43 (7)
ES	10* (10)	0* (10)	0* (11)	13* (8)	0* (4)	64 (11)	–	86 (7)	50 (8)	60 (5)	0* (5)	50 (2)	60 (5)	50 (4)	57 (7)
IT	13* (8)	0* (9)	0* (9)	0* (7)	0* (4)	56 (9)	78 (9)	–	71 (7)	50 (4)	0* (5)	50 (2)	60 (5)	50 (4)	50 (6)
DE	15* (13)	0* (10)	7* (14)	13* (8)	0* (4)	69 (13)	45 (11)	56 (9)	–	60 (5)	0* (5)	50 (2)	40 (5)	25 (4)	57 (7)
CH	14 (7)	0* (7)	14 (7)	0* (6)	0 (3)	86 (7)	57 (7)	33 (6)	71 (7)	–	0* (4)	0 (1)	25 (4)	25 (4)	20 (5)
ZA	29 (7)	71 (7)	86 (7)	50 (6)	75 (4)	29 (7)	0* (7)	0* (7)	14 (7)	17 (6)	–	0 (2)	0* (5)	0* (4)	0* (5)
SK	25 (4)	0* (4)	0* (4)	0* (4)	0* (4)	50 (4)	75 (4)	50 (4)	50 (4)	33 (3)	0* (4)	–	50 (2)	0 (1)	50 (2)
BR	17 (6)	17 (6)	0* (6)	0* (5)	0 (3)	33 (6)	50 (6)	67 (6)	33 (6)	20 (5)	0* (6)	33 (3)	–	100* (4)	60 (5)
IN	14 (7)	29 (7)	14 (7)	0* (5)	0 (3)	14 (7)	50 (6)	67 (6)	17 (6)	17 (6)	0* (6)	33 (3)	100* (5)	–	50 (4)
JP	40 (10)	10* (10)	0* (10)	25 (8)	0* (4)	50 (10)	56 (9)	38 (8)	67 (9)	43 (7)	14 (7)	50 (4)	50 (6)	29 (7)	–

Notes

This table (from Nobes and Stadler, 2013) reports the results of a meta-analysis of the classification studies of Table 4.1. The bottom-left triangle considers all 16 classifications, and the top-right triangle considers the intrinsic classifications (i.e. excluding studies 2, 3, 4, 10, 14 and 15). For each country-pair, the table shows the frequency (in %) with which the country-pair is classified in the same group. The number in brackets (N) indicates in how many classifications both countries of the country-pair were included. * indicates that the percentage for the country-pair is significantly different from 50% at the 5% level (two-sided, based on a test of proportion); the test requires at least two observations, i.e. the country-pair needs to be included in at least two classifications; a significant result indicates a high degree of confidence that the relationship of the countries in the pair (either being or not being grouped together) is not arbitrary. The countries are: US (United States), Australia (AU), United Kingdom (UK), Canada (CA), Hong Kong (HK), France (FR), Spain (ES), Italy (IT), Germany (DE), Switzerland (CH), South Africa (ZA), South Korea (SK), Brazil (BR), India (IN) and Japan (JP). For those classification studies of Table 4.1 which provide more than one classification, we only use one/the main classification, as follows: for classification study 7, p. 433 (1975 analysis, measurement practices); for 9, Table 8 (we use the two-group classification, not the more detailed one); for 12, Table 1 (again we use the two-group classification, not the more detailed one of Table 2); for 13, Figure 2 (multidimensional scaling); for 15, Table 3, Panel C; for 16, Table 4 (principal component analysis).

shows that those countries were together for 40 per cent of the ten classifications which included them both. Scores of 0 per cent or 100 per cent reveal consensus among the classifications. The table also shows which percentages for country-pairs are significantly different from 50 per cent, based on a test of proportion (two-sided). A significant result indicates a high degree of confidence that the relationship of the countries in the pair (either being or not being grouped together) is not arbitrary. Although the various classifications consider different numbers of countries and result in different numbers of groups,[2] our method of analysing country-pairs allows the combination of these different classifications into a meta-analysis.

The meta-analysis can be summarised as showing two main features. First, most of the percentages for the country-pairs are not significantly different from 50 per cent,[3] which suggests a high degree of arbitrariness in the classifications; however, many relationships are not arbitrary. Similar conclusions can be drawn from observing that there are many scores from 33 to 67 per cent. For example, the results for Italy in the bottom-left triangle reveal that there is little consensus concerning which countries it should be classified with (because there are no percentages above 50 per cent which are statistically significant). On the other hand, there is strong consensus that Italy should *not* be classified with 'Anglo' countries (see the six percentages below 50 per cent which are statistically significant). Similar remarks apply to France, Spain and Germany. Second, a British group can be identified, which includes Australia and Hong Kong (see the UK column and row in the bottom-left triangle). However, North America is not included in that group: the first column of Table 8.1 shows that only Canada has usually been classified with the United States. The first row (intrinsic classifications only) shows an even lower tendency for there to be an 'Anglo-American' group.

Several caveats must be entered about this meta-analysis. First, it uses data (i.e. the classifications) spanning several decades, during which countries might have changed their relationships. This and other reasons might mean that the various results should not have been combined. Nevertheless, to the extent that certain pairs of countries retain their relative positions over many decades (even surviving a move to IFRS) suggests that the classifications are picking up something fundamental. However, whether the insights from this analysis can be relied upon at all depends greatly on whether there are biased errors in the data or the methods used by the previous classifiers. This is a central issue of this chapter, so we return to the worth of Table 8.1 after we have summarised that issue.

8.2 Factors affecting classification

Early accounting classifications seem to have been affected by the national backgrounds of the classifiers or of the data gatherers. We have suggested, especially in Chapter 6, ways in which classification has also been affected by the data used. First, the choice of which characteristics to measure has a profound effect on the results. Once chosen, the way of measuring the characteristics has varied: several classifiers apparently used no data, some used incoherent data (mixtures of rules and impressions of practices) and others used data which are arguably of limited practical relevance (differences in rules). Many classifiers did not specify the scope of the objects being classified (e.g. large or listed companies) or the date.

However, some classifiers have entered caveats. Frank (1979, p. 596) noted that the topics included in his PW data vary in importance. Frank did not make a selection or comment on the mixture of rules and impressions of practices in the data, but warned that the coding scheme which turns that mixture into data for classification might introduce errors. Nair and Frank (1980) noted that their classifications differed if based on presentation topics rather than on measurement topics. D'Arcy (2001, p. 333) pointed out that different topics would lead to different classifications, and noted the inherent problem of using data on rules instead of practices. Nobes (2011) mentioned the need for judgement in identifying important characteristics, and excludes some characteristics on these grounds.

We can now return to the meta-analysis of Table 8.1. We have noted above that the early classifiers might have been particularly aware of US and UK differences, and that many subsequent classifications were based on PW data which had been originally designed to reveal such differences. This could explain why no 'Anglo-American' group was generally found.

The lessons for accounting researchers are that (i) a classification should be based on detailed observation of characteristics, (ii) the characteristics chosen should ideally be informed by the purpose of the classification, and at least be deliberately chosen and overt, (iii) related to this, any claims of objectivity are incoherent, (iv) accounting practices are a better representation of an 'accounting system' than rules are and (v) the set of companies included in the accounting 'system' and the period of the data should be clearly specified. It is further clear from this survey that the effect of inclusions or exclusions of countries, sectors (especially financial and extractive) and characteristics needs to be empirically investigated in order to see whether classification is robust to manipulation of these issues or whether it is instead essentially arbitrary. We now proceed with that.

8.3 Data for an experiment

The rest of this chapter reports on experiments using data on IFRS practices as reported by Nobes and Stadler (2013). The sample included companies from the world's largest economies which used IFRS in 2011, as follows: (i) the countries with the six largest stock markets where IFRS was required from 2005 (i.e. Australia, France, Germany, Italy, Spain and the UK), (ii) the two other countries with large stock markets with a longer history of IFRS usage (South Africa and Switzerland), (iii) Canada and South Korea, where IFRS has been recently adopted, and (iv) Hong Kong and companies from China which use IFRS.[4] In order to include Canada and South Korea, we used financial statements from

2011 onwards. In particular, we used company reports for years ended 31 December 2011 (or latest before) for 12 countries.[5] Our sample included the largest listed companies in each of these jurisdictions,[6] which comprised 65 per cent of the total market capitalisation of these countries.[7] Companies with foreign influence or which were subsidiaries were excluded. In total, we examined the IFRS practices of 516 companies. Details of the sample are provided in Appendix III.

Table 8.2 shows the sample by country and sector. We wish to investigate whether exclusion of certain sectors might affect classification. Prior literature indicates that the financial and extractive sectors have idiosyncratic policies.[8] Given the topic of this book, we should admit that the classification of companies by sector exhibits the difficulties typical of classification. There are several accepted versions. We chose the 'Industry Classification Benchmark' (ICB) of the index company FTSE. The corresponding data were from Worldscope (data code WC07040). Consistently with our recommended approach, we used judgement to adjust it for our purposes, in particular to calculate country totals for extractive companies.[9]

We concluded above that practices are the best representation of an accounting system. We record the IFRS practices of companies and use them as the characteristics to be measured in order to classify a country. Even for companies which are fully complying with IFRS, there is considerable scope for varied practice because, for example: (i) the recognition of expenses (e.g. impairments) or assets (e.g. development projects) relies on the exercise of judgement against somewhat vague criteria, (ii) the measurement of liabilities (e.g. provisions) or assets (e.g. the fair value of investment properties) involves estimation, and (iii) many standards offer choices to companies. The first two of these are hard to assess (although, see an attempt by Wehrfritz *et al.*, 2012), but data on the third can be hand-picked from the annual reports of companies. These data provide a good indication of the influence of factors such as country and industry because the differences in practices are caused by management choices and not by regulations.

The list of policy topics used by Kvaal and Nobes (2010) is shown here as Table 8.3, after deleting the topics on which choice was removed from IFRS by 2011. There are eight presentation topics and six measurement topics. For the last two topics in the table, changes to IFRS had already been made by 2011 but were not compulsory for any of our companies.[10] Kvaal and Nobes (2012) found that there was little early adoption of IFRS changes, but we report on this below. For financial companies, Kvaal and Nobes (2010) omitted topics on which there were sector-specific presentation practices influenced by pre-IFRS laws. We do not do that, because part of our purpose is to investigate the effects of including or excluding certain sectors. Still, we omit five topics for financial companies because they are not appropriate for the sector, as explained in Appendix IV.

When the purpose of research is to investigate whether IFRS policy choices are associated with country, then it is appropriate to examine as many policy topics as are observable. However, as discussed in earlier chapters, for assessing a country's

Table 8.2 Sample by country and sector

Sector	AU	UK	CA	CN	HK	FR	ES	IT	DE	CH	ZA	SK	Σ
0/1 Extractives	6	9	21	7	0	2	1	1	0	0	7	3	57
0/1 Other oil and gas, basic materials	4	3	2	3	0	2	3	0	7	3	1	4	32
2 Industrials	7	15	2	12	4	9	8	7	6	2	6	13	91
3 Consumer goods	2	10	2	3	3	7	1	5	7	3	2	5	50
4 Health care	2	3	0	1	0	2	1	1	2	4	2	0	18
5 Consumer services	8	20	8	4	3	7	3	8	6	0	6	4	77
6 Telecommunications	1	4	3	1	1	1	1	1	1	0	2	3	20
7 Utilities	1	5	1	3	3	2	4	3	2	0	0	2	26
8 Financials	20	22	10	13	8	6	9	12	6	6	6	11	129
9 Technology	0	2	0	2	0	2	1	0	2	1	0	4	14
Σ	51	93	49	49	22	40	32	38	39	20	32	49	514

Notes
This table reports descriptive statistics of the sample companies. The countries are Australia (AU), United Kingdom (UK), Canada (CA), China (CN), Hong Kong (HK), France (FR), Spain (ES), Italy (IT), Germany (DE), Switzerland (CH), South Africa (ZA) and South Korea (SK). Sector is according to the first digit of the Industry Classification Benchmark (ICB), except that we show all the extractive companies (sectors 0530 and 1770; subsectors 1753 and 1755; Fortescue Metals Group) together in the first row, and all the remaining companies of sector 0 (oil and gas) and sector 1 (basic materials) together in the second row.

Table 8.3 IFRS policy topics

Topic	IFRS policy options	Standard[b]
1[a]	• income statement by nature – by function or neither	IAS 1.99
2[a]	• no inclusion of a line for EBIT or operating profit – line included	IAS 1.82
3	• equity accounting results included in 'operating' – immediately after, or after 'finance'	IAS 1.82[c]
4	• balance sheet showing net assets – showing assets=credits	IAS 1.54[c]
5	• balance sheet with liquidity decreasing (cash at top) – liquidity increasing	IAS 1.54[c]
6	• indirect operating cash flows – direct	IAS 7.18
7	• dividends received shown as operating cash flow – not	IAS 7.31
8[a]	• interest paid shown as operating cash flow – not	IAS 7.31
9	• some property at fair value – only cost	IAS 16.29
10	• investment property at fair value – at cost	IAS 40.30
11[a]	• some designation of financial instruments at fair value – none	IAS 39.9
12[a]	• FIFO only for inventory cost – weighted average used	IAS 2.25
13	• actuarial gains and losses to OCI – corridor method or to income in full	IAS 19.92/3
14	• proportionate consolidation of joint ventures – equity method	IAS 31.30

Notes

a=not appropriate, and therefore not collected for financial companies.

b=versions of the standards ruling in 2011.

c=IAS 1 specifies lists of items to be shown in financial statements, but does not specify their order. This table shows 14 IFRS policy topics on which choices were observable in 2011. Topics 1 to 8 are presentation issues and topics 9 to 14 are measurement issues. The topics are as in Kvaal and Nobes (2010). Most topics are binary choices but topics 1, 3 and 13 allow a choice between three options. For these, we define binary choices: for topic 1, we distinguish whether or not the income statement is by nature because the 'neither' cases are usually more similar to 'by function' than 'by nature'; for topic 3, we consider the key issue to be whether or not the item is included in operating profit; for topic 13, we combine the options 'corridor method' and 'to income in full' because we consider the key issue to be whether or not actuarial gains and losses are ever charged in the income statement, which is not the case under 'actuarial gains and losses to OCI'.

accounting 'system' or a country's profile of IFRS practices, judgement is needed to exclude (or give lower weight to) topics likely to be of little importance to users of financial statements (e.g. the liquidity order of assets in a balance sheet). We investigate the sensitivity of classifications to such exclusion of topics.

Appendix IV provides details about the data collection and the coding procedures used to generate binary choice data from the 14 IFRS policy topics. The empirical analyses below are based on a total of 5,689 hand-picked IFRS policy choices of the 514 companies from 12 countries.

8.4 Findings on policy choice

Table 8.4 reports, by country, the percentages of companies in our sample which chose particular options. For several topics, the policy choice was observable for all 514 companies. However, we only count companies for which the policy is observable, which explains why the 'N' in Table 8.4 is smaller for certain topics, notably investment property measurement (topic 10).

Table 8.4 Percentages of policy choice by country and topic

IFRS policy choice	N	AU	UK	CA	CN	HK	FR	ES	IT	DE	CH	ZA	SK
1 Income statement by nature	385	35	11	5	44	36	29	96	81	24	29	15	3
2 Operating profit not shown	385	42	1	31	31	29	3	0	0	12	0	0	0
3 Equity profits in operating	423	59	35	48	4	0	8	23	14	35	39	7	4
4 Balance sheet showing net assets	514	100	76	0	39	82	0	0	0	0	5	0	0
5 Balance sheet with liquidity decreasing	514	100	10	100	24	14	10	22	29	26	50	9	98
6 Indirect cash flows	514	4	98	100	98	100	100	91	95	100	95	66	100
7 Dividends received as operating	348	87	37	85	5	30	79	39	20	71	43	86	91
8 Interest paid as operating	381	86	61	74	44	43	79	52	69	61	64	96	89
9 Some property at fair value	504	10	10	2	0	5	0	0	0	0	0	0	0
10 Investment property at fair value	216	93	68	36	21	94	20	5	0	5	80	40	3
11 Some fair value designation	383	10	3	13	0	7	24	4	4	6	7	23	19
12 FIFO only	329	21	42	23	6	15	11	22	19	0	36	23	6
13 Actuarial gains/losses to OCI	414	85	89	72	8	36	60	68	30	59	35	28	83
14 Proportionate consolidation of JVs	379	6	25	55	9	0	71	70	38	17	43	59	17

Notes

This table reports the percentages of companies per country and topic which make the respective IFRS policy choice in 2011. The countries are as in Table 8.2. N is the number of observations/companies. See Table 8.3 and Appendix IV for details of the topics.

As explained earlier, some previous researchers observed an association between policy choice and sector. Significant differences between sectors were evident when we split the entire sample into three sectors: financial, extractive and other. Table 8.5 shows particularly clear examples. More importantly for this chapter, there are also significant differences between the sectors within countries. As may be seen, compared to other companies in their countries, Australian financial companies prefer fair value for investment properties, Canadian financial companies prefer not to recognise actuarial gains/losses as OCI (they prefer the corridor method), Canadian extractive companies prefer to proportionally consolidate joint ventures, and British financial companies are less likely to show net assets but more likely to start the balance sheet with cash. In all these cases, a χ^2 test of independence shows that a null hypothesis of no association with sector can be rejected at the 1 per cent level. These are examples of how a country's sectoral mix might affect its mean scores on topics, which might then affect classification, as examined in the next section.

8.5 Sensitivity of classifications

As recorded in Chapter 6, several different statistical methods of classification have been employed by previous researchers. We begin with principal component analysis. Table 8.6 shows the principal components for one version of the data: all 14 topics for all sectors of all 12 countries. This analysis leads to a three-group initial classification, summarised as 'run' 1 in Table 8.7. In this table, we report the results for 11 different versions of the data. For ease of comparison, Germany is always shown in Group 1.

The Kaiser–Meyer–Olkin (KMO) measure of sampling adequacy should be higher than 0.6 (or possibly 0.5) for the data to be considered suitable for factor analysis (Kaiser, 1970, 1974). Run 1 has a low KMO. However, by excluding China, Switzerland and South Korea (for reasons explained below), the KMO improves greatly (see run 2). However, although the KMO can change substantially due to the exclusion of countries, the classifications are generally not affected (see below). We therefore conclude that, for our purposes, there is no need to be concerned about analyses which show a low KMO. Nevertheless, the majority of our runs has a KMO of above 0.6.

Excluding countries

Before the analysis (below) of the effects of excluding topics and sectors, we experimented by excluding various countries (i.e. the objects being classified). In Chapter 2, it was noted that this can affect classification. For example, Pluto is no longer classified as a planet because of the increased number of objects being classified after the discovery of bodies larger than Pluto with orbits further from the sun. We also pointed out that the clustering programs can be affected by which countries are included. We start here by excluding China (for which, all our sample companies are listed on the Hong Kong exchange), South Africa

Table 8.5 Examples of sectoral differences in policy choice

Country	IFRS policy choice	N	% financials	% extractives	% others	p-value
All	10 Investment property at fair value	216	61	0	9	<0.01
All	13 Actuarial gains/losses to OCI	414	39	58	73	<0.01
All	14 Proportionate consolidation of JVs	379	27	56	35	<0.01
AU	10 Investment property at fair value	15	100	–	50	<0.01
CA	13 Actuarial gains/losses to OCI	39	10	82	100	<0.01
CA	14 Proportionate consolidation of JVs	38	30	82	36	0.01
UK	4 Balance sheet showing net assets	93	45	67	89	<0.01
UK	5 Balance sheet with liquidity decreasing	93	32	0	3	<0.01

Notes
This table reports the percentages of financial, extractive and other companies which make the respective IFRS policy choice in 2011. N is the number of observations/companies. The column 'p-value' reports the p-values for χ^2 tests of independence. See Table 8.2 for the definition and frequencies of financial and extractive companies. See Table 8.3 and Appendix IV for details of the topics.

Table 8.6 Principal component analysis using all available data

Country	Component 1	Component 2	Component 3
AU	**0.1764**	0.1520	−0.6277
UK	0.0978	**0.4717**	−0.1518
CA	**0.4662**	−0.1047	−0.1532
CN	−0.0320	**0.4829**	0.2698
HK	−0.0829	**0.6540**	−0.0987
FR	**0.3580**	−0.0139	0.1950
ES	0.1798	0.0360	**0.4511**
IT	0.1531	0.1304	**0.4571**
DE	**0.3719**	0.0456	0.0757
CH	**0.2574**	0.2319	−0.0023
ZA	**0.3714**	−0.0467	0.0344
SK	**0.4557**	−0.0774	−0.1399

Notes
This table reports the results of principal component analysis using data on the IFRS policy choices made on 14 topics by companies of all sectors from 12 countries in 2011. The data used are the percentages shown in Table 8.4. Specifically, the countries constitute the variables (i.e. the objects of study) and the IFRS policy choices constitute the observations. The numbers shown are the principal component loadings after varimax rotation. Principal components are those with eigenvalues greater than one. Bold numbers indicate the component on which the respective country loads the most. The countries are as in Table 8.2.

(where many listed companies are influenced from the UK)[11] and Switzerland (where IFRS is not required, and for which we have the smallest sample).

However, the exclusion of one or more countries does not have a large effect on the groupings of the remaining countries (based on principal component analysis), as a study of Table 8.7 shows. For example, there is no change when two countries are excluded (moving from run 3 to run 4), or when other countries are gradually added (from run 4 to run 5, then run 6). However, exclusion of *three* countries (when moving from run 1 to run 2) changes the grouping of France, although it now associates with more than one group. Furthermore, it is also possible to find effects of excluding a country on the more detailed classifications in dendrogram form. For example, Figures 8.1 and 8.2 show the dendrograms resulting from runs 5 and 6. The only difference in the data is that South Africa is added in run 6; but this causes the position of Switzerland to change. It would therefore be possible for researchers to arrive at different classifications of country X by including or excluding country Y. This might be done deliberately, subconsciously or accidentally. It would be possible for researchers to rationalise the selection of countries, and thereby affect the result.

Excluding topics

The selection of topics/characteristics fundamentally affects the classifications: in effect, the topic scores are being classified, as they are the proxies for the countries. An example from Chapter 2 is that the original Linnaean classification of plants chose to ignore everything but reproductive features, but was

Table 8.7 Grouping of countries based on principal component analysis, varying the countries, topics and sectors included

Run #	Topics	Sectors	AU	UK	CA	CN	HK	FR	ES	IT	DE	CH	ZA	SK	KMO
1	All	All	1(2)	2	1	2	2		3	3	1	1(2)	1	1	0.3400
2	All	All	1	2	1	—	2	3(1)	3	3	1	—	—	1	0.7156
3	Excluding 2, 5, 7	All	2	2	1	—	2	—	1	1	1	—	—	1	0.5285
4	Excluding 2, 5, 7	All	2	2	—	—	2	—	1	1	1	—	—	—	0.6086
5	Excluding 2, 5, 7	All	2	2	—	—	2	—	1	1	1	1(2)	—	—	0.6770
6	Excluding 2, 5, 7	All	2	2	—	—	2	—	1	1	1	1(2)	1	—	0.2723
7	Excluding 2, 4, 5, 7	All	2	2	2(1)	—	2	—	1	1	1	—	—	1[2]	0.3132
8	Excluding 2, 5, 7	Excluding F	2	2	—	—	2	—	1	1	1	—	—	—	0.7376
9	Excluding 2, 5, 7	Excluding F and E	2	2	—	—	2	—	1	1	1	—	—	—	0.7227
10	Excluding 2, 4, 5, 7	Excluding F	2	2(1)	1	2	1	—	1	1	1	—	—	1[2]	0.5464
11	All	Excluding F and E	3	2	1(3)	2	2	—	1	1[2]	1	1	1	1(3)	0.7294

Notes

This table reports groupings of countries based on principal component analysis using data on IFRS policy choices in 2011. The countries, topics and sectors included vary between each 'run'. Each country is grouped according to the principal component (after varimax rotation) on which it loads the most. Principal components are those with eigenvalues greater than one. The number of principal components and therefore the number of groups differs between the runs. The numbers 1, 2 and 3 in the columns headed by the two-letter country acronyms denote the different groups. For ease of comparison, Germany is always shown in Group 1. A number in brackets (square brackets) denotes the group of the principal component on which the country loads second highest and is shown if the difference between the highest and second highest loading is below 0.05 (0.10), i.e. if the grouping of the country is not very clear. See Table 8.6 for details on the principal component analysis of run 1. 'KMO' denotes the Kaiser-Meyer-Olkin measure of sampling adequacy. The countries are as in Table 8.2. In the column 'Sectors', 'F' denotes the financial sector and 'E' denotes the extractive sector. See Table 8.2 for the definition and frequencies of financial and extractive companies. See Table 8.3 and Appendix IV for details of the topics.

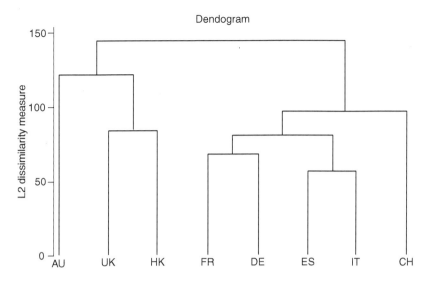

Figure 8.1 Dendrogram for run 5.

Note
This figure shows the dendrogram of hierarchical clustering using the average linkage method for run 5. See Table 8.7 for details of the specification of run 5.

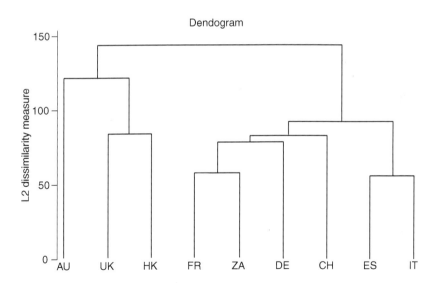

Figure 8.2 Dendrogram for run 6.

Note
This figure shows the dendrogram of hierarchical clustering using the average linkage method for run 6. See Table 8.7 for details of the specification of run 6.

substantially revised when DNA evidence became available. Let us consider the implications of this by taking the example of Canada, which adopted IFRS in 2011 and which has therefore not been classified before by IFRS practices. One researcher (possibly from France) might hypothesise that Canada would be grouped with France, because French is an official language and because code law is practised in a major province (Québec). The researcher could find support for this prediction by focusing on run 3 of Table 8.7. However, another researcher (possibly from the UK) might hypothesise that Canada should be grouped with the UK. This could be supported by focusing on run 7.

The difference in classification emerges by excluding one topic (topic 4: does the balance sheet show net assets?). Canadian companies all follow the French approach of not showing net assets. If one were to try to decide which of runs 3 or 7 produces the more meaningful grouping, one would have to face at least two questions: (i) Is topic 4 important for describing a country's accounting system? (ii) Does the choice of Canadian companies result from 'French-ness'? When deciding on (i), we note that the presentation choice does not change any accounting number. When deciding on (ii), we note that most of our Canadian companies are listed in the US[12] and that practice there[13] happens to be the same as French practice under IFRS. Neither of the classifications is 'wrong'. Therefore, the point is a good example of the old insight that no classifications are 'real'. As noted above, different researchers could arrive at different classifications using the same data.

Although no classifications are 'real', some are perhaps more reasonable than others. At the least, researchers should not abdicate responsibility for choosing the characteristics, and they should make their choices overt. We have shown that some accounting classifiers have not complied with those desiderata. For the purposes of this chapter (i.e. investigating sensitivity), we do not need to conclude on what is the best answer. However, one could take the view that the exclusion of several presentation topics increases the meaningfulness of a classification because it stresses the more important topics. For example, we can compare runs 2 and 3 (in Table 8.7). They are both for all sectors of the same nine countries, but run 3's exclusion of the three presentation topics deemed unimportant in Nobes (2011) causes Australia to move into Group 2 (with the UK and Hong Kong), and France, Spain and Italy to join Germany in Group 1. If a further topic (topic 4) which does not affect measurement (or even the size of any total) is excluded as in run 7, then Canada also joins the 'Anglo-Saxon' group. This illustrates the above point: Nobes (2011), as reported in Chapter 7, would not have been able to show that the two-class accounting world had survived for 30 years if he had chosen a different topic mix. However, we repeat that such judgements are inevitable when classifying in any discipline.

Using our data, after all the 'unimportant' topics are excluded, the multidimensional scaling (MDS) result is as in Figure 8.3, which shows the 'Anglo' countries on the right-hand side. The dendrogram for the same data is shown as Figure 8.4, although this presents a confused picture because of the way in which clustering works (see Section 6.1).

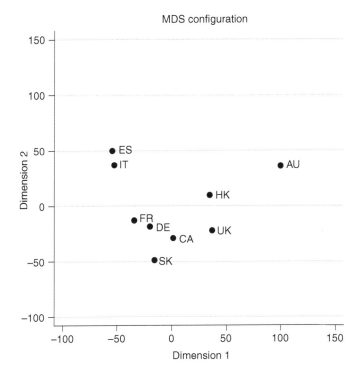

Figure 8.3 Multidimensional scaling for run 7.

Note
This figure shows the results of classical multidimensional scaling for run 7. The Mardia measure is 86.28%. See Table 8.6 for details of the specification of run 7.

Excluding sectors

The effect of excluding sectors can be illustrated in several ways. Comparison of runs 4, 8 and 9 in Table 8.7 shows that there is not necessarily any effect of such exclusions. All three runs relate to the 11 'important' topics and to seven countries which result in a clear two-group classification using all sectors.[14] First one sector, then two are excluded, but the two groups remain stable. However, the exclusion of a sector *can* have an effect. For example, when the financial sector is excluded by moving from run 7 to run 10, it causes Canada and Hong Kong to leave Australia and the UK. Moving from run 1 to run 11 shows the effect of excluding two sectors: Australia creates a group with South Korea, and the Italy/Spain group disappears.

The exclusion of sectors should not be done lightly. The financial and extractive sectors are very important in several countries (see Table 8.2). Excluding both of them amounts to ignoring more than half of the accounting 'system' for Australia and Canada, or one-third for the UK. Furthermore, much of the international variation (e.g. in the use of fair value) is located in these sectors.

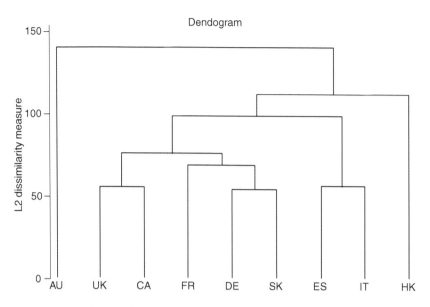

Figure 8.4 Dendrogram for run 7.

Note
This figure shows the dendrogram of hierarchical clustering using the average linkage method for run 7. See Table. 8.7 for details of the specification of run 7.

8.6 How the countries are grouped

Although vital effects can result from exclusion of topics, and noticeable effects from exclusion of countries or sectors, certain aspects of the classifications are remarkably stable. For example: (a) Italy and Spain are always in the same group, sometimes by themselves, (b) Germany and France are generally in the same group, (c) the UK, Hong Kong and China are generally in the same group and (d) the UK is never with Germany, France, Italy and Spain. Figure 8.5 shows the classification based on multidimensional scaling (MDS) for all countries and all topics, but excluding financial and extractive companies (run 11).

Jurisdictions which were not classified on the basis of IFRS practices in Chapter 7 are Canada, China, Hong Kong, South Africa, South Korea and Switzerland. Three of these (China, Hong Kong and South Korea) had not been included in any of the previous intrinsic classifications. In this present study, Switzerland is never with the UK but, predictably, is generally with Germany and France. South Korea is also generally with Germany, which is the position of Japan (which has influenced Korea) in previous classifications. Interestingly, despite South Africa's partially British heritage, it is always with Germany and never with the UK. However, like South Korea, South Africa has a version of Roman law. Hong Kong and China are nearly always shown with the UK. This is not surprising, given that Hong Kong's pre-IFRS accounting system was

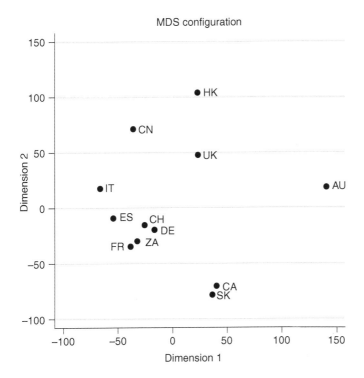

Figure 8.5 Multidimensional scaling for run 11.

Note
This figure shows the results of classical multidimensional scaling for run 11. The Mardia measure is 90.93%. See Table 8.7 for details of the specification of run 11.

closely modelled on the UK's, and that all the Chinese companies in our sample are listed on the Hong Kong stock exchange. Canada cannot be classified unambiguously.

Our data could be used to support the frequently used split between common law and code law countries. For example, by focusing on runs 4, 5, 7, 8 and 9 of Table 8.7, we could show a 100 per cent correlation between that split and our two groupings of countries by IFRS practices. The same would apply to run 6 if South Africa is scored as having 'Roman Dutch' law (as in legal classifications) rather than as 'English origin' (as in La Porta *et al.*, 1998). However, if we focused on runs 2, 10 and 11, quite a different story could be told. This is a further illustration of the need for judgement by researchers and caution by readers.

8.7 Conclusions of this chapter and this book

Classification is a fundamental activity in many scientific disciplines and in everyday work in several fields. There are indications that classifications in several fields have strongly reflected their classifiers. This was particularly obvious in the way in which man originally classified himself and his world. Although some independence can be achieved by detailed systematic observation, the choice of characteristics to represent the objects being classified remains inevitably a matter of judgement. For example, even though Linnaeus' botanical classification rested on meticulous observation, he chose to ignore most of the observable things about plants. Classifications can still be useful even when arbitrary, though some classifications are now described by biologists as 'natural' rather than arbitrary. Whether a classification is useful or not is related to its purpose. We collated lessons from other fields in preparation for analysing the long history of classification in international accounting.

Accounting classifications have been extensively referred to in policy-making debates; and they have been used as part of the setting for research on many topics, and as a source of independent variables in empirical research. If the classifications are inappropriate, or have been used inappropriately, the settings or variables are wrong. However, few accounting classifiers have discussed or investigated the robustness of classification to variations in such matters as the number of objects classified and the nature of the characteristics chosen to represent the objects. In our survey of previous accounting classifications, we find a wide range on these matters.

Table 8.8 is a simplified version of Table 4.1, to act as a reminder of the classifications studied in this book. Like early classifications in other fields, the early accounting classifications (items 1 to 4 of Table 8.8) seem to reflect the backgrounds of the classifiers. For example, Americans saw a three-class world: US, UK and other. Another point from above is that classification should be based on observation. However, those early accounting classifications did not use data. Other classifications (items 9 to 11) were also not based on detailed systematic observation but on informal impressions. From the late 1970s, several classifiers (items 5 to 8 and 12 and 13) did use data, but the data were based on the opinions of others. In terms of the discussion in Chapter 2, the evidence was hearsay. None of the classifiers appears to have looked for, or corrected, errors in their databases.

Most accounting classifiers did not address the fact that a classification depends entirely on the characteristics chosen to represent the countries being classified. Classifications 5 to 8 even used data that had been designed to reveal US/UK differences, whereupon the classifications reflected this. Most classifications do not specify their date or the type of companies considered. Where the latter is specified, the scope is listed companies. Nearly all classifiers have ignored sectoral differences, and none had investigated the effect of such differences on classifications.

This chapter shows that classification is highly susceptible to the characteristics used to measure the objects classified. However, the classifications are fairly robust to the inclusion/exclusion of countries and sectors.

Table 8.8 Features of some classifications

Researchers	No. of countries	Type of data	Classification method
1 Hatfield, 1911	4	Impressions of practices	Judgement
2 Mueller, 1967	5	Impressions of purposes	Judgement
3 Seidler, 1967	7	Impressions of influences	Judgement
4 AAA, 1977	6	Impressions of influences	Judgement
5 da Costa et al., 1978	38	Mixture of rules and impressions of practices (by Price Waterhouse partners)	PCA
6 Frank, 1979	38	As above	PCA, MDS
7 Nair and Frank, 1980	38, 46	As above	PCA, SSA
8 Goodrich, 1982	64	Impressions of concepts (by Price Waterhouse partners)	PCA
9 Nobes, 1983b	14	Impressions of practices	PCA
10 Puxty et al., 1987	4	Impressions of regulatory style	Judgement
11 Shoenthal, 1989	2	Impressions of competencies of auditors	Judgement
12 Doupnik and Salter, 1993	50	Impressions of practices (by academics and auditors)	Average-linkage clustering
13 D'Arcy, 2001	15	Rules	Clustering, MDS
14 Leuz et al., 2003	31	Facts and impressions relating to stock markets and investor protection	Clustering by k-means
15 Leuz, 2010	49	Facts and impressions on legal system, securities regulation	Clustering by k-means
16 Nobes, 2011	8	Practices	PCA, MDS, clustering

Key
PCA = principal component analysis; MDS = multidimensional scaling; SSA = smallest space analysis.

Notes

1 This chapter is based on work done with Christian Stadler, which appeared as Nobes and Stadler (2013).

2 In two of the classifications (Nobes (1983b) and Doupnik and Salter (1993)), countries were first divided into two groups, and those were subdivided further. For the meta-analysis, we used the two-group classifications (see Table 8.2 note), which stress similarities rather than differences. Compared to using the multi-group classifications, this increases the scores in Table 8.1 for several country-pairs.

3 A total of 61 per cent of the scores in the bottom-left triangle and 75 per cent in the top-right triangle (64 out of 105 country-pairs and 76 out of 101 country-pairs, respectively; only 101 country-pairs are considered for the top-right triangle because there are four cases where the country-pair is only included in one classification but the test requires at least two observations). The main reason for the lower frequency of significant scores in the top-right triangle is the reduced power of the tests due to considering fewer classifications.

4 Although China has not fully adopted IFRS, the majority of the largest listed Chinese companies prepares IFRS financial statements, because they are listed on the Hong Kong Stock Exchange (HKEx), which required IFRS from 2005. Consequently, Chinese companies with a listing in Hong Kong and Mainland China prepared two sets of financial statements (IFRS and Chinese GAAP). However, from 2010, HKEx accepts Chinese GAAP financial statements, and six companies in our sample have stopped preparing IFRS financial statements.

5 The one exception to this is that we include the first available IFRS financial statements for ten Canadian and four South Korean companies which have year-ends other than 31 December 2011. This enables the inclusion of six Canadian and four South Korean financial companies; in particular, our Canadian sample would otherwise not include any *bank* because all Canadian banks in our sample have 31 October year-ends.

6 Findings of country influence would probably be even stronger for smaller companies because of less international influence (Nobes and Perramon, 2013).

7 According to Worldscope data for 2011 (Worldscope code: WC07210).

8 Christensen and Nikolaev (2013) show that real-estate firms (which are part of the financial sector) choose to use fair value for investment property more frequently than other firms. Jafaar and McLeay (2007, p. 180) refer to special practices in the extractive industries.

9 We define extractive companies as those in sector 0530 (oil and gas producers), sector 1770 (mining), subsector 1753 (aluminium) and subsector 1755 (non-ferrous metals); additionally, we classify Fortescue Metals Group of subsector 1757 (iron and steel) as an extractive company. We believe that using ICB codes results in a better industry classification than using primary SIC codes (Worldscope data code: WC07021). If using SIC codes, we would identify extractive companies as 'mining' (SIC codes starting with the digits 10, 12, 13 or 14) and financial companies as 'finance, insurance and real estate' (SIC codes starting with the digit 6). Using ICB codes, we classify 57 (129) companies as extractive (financial), and using SIC codes we would have classified 79 per cent (94 per cent) in the same way. The main difference is that many integrated oil and gas companies (e.g. BP) are not classified as extractive but as 'manufacturing' using SIC codes due to their petroleum refining businesses. Additionally, the classification of some companies using SIC codes is unsuitable for our purposes: e.g. China Oilfield Services is classified as an extractive company even though it does no extraction.

10 IAS 19 was amended in 2011 to remove the option on the treatment of actuarial gains and losses. IAS 31 was replaced in 2011, thus removing the option for proportional consolidation. Both changes were only compulsory for 2013 onwards.

11 As for all countries, we excluded companies with foreign influence (see Appendix III).

12 Specifically, 35 of the 49 Canadian companies in our sample were listed in the US at the end of 2011. We define 'listed in the US' as filing 10–K or 40–F reports with the Securities and Exchange Commission (SEC). The corresponding data is collected from the EDGAR database of the SEC.

13 See, for example, AICPA (2010, p. 147). There were no format requirements in Canadian GAAP, although almost universal practice was to present 'total assets' as in the US (Ordelheide and KPMG, 2001, p. 552).

14 The five countries of Kvaal and Nobes (2010), plus Italy (which groups with Spain) and Hong Kong (which groups with the UK).

Appendix I
Classification of languages

The classification shown here in diagrammatic form is based on Bloomfield (1935). It is not supposed to be exhaustive, and is more detailed in some parts than in others.

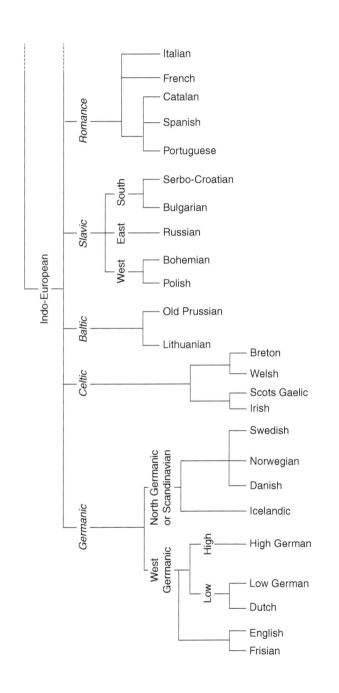

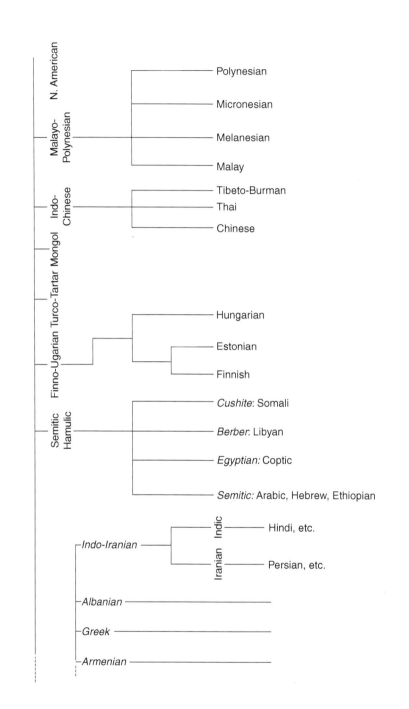

Appendix II

An extension of the classification hypothesis

The figure below is an expanded version of the corrected 1979 hypothesis. It is not intended to be seen as reliable but as summarising various findings of the research of the writer and others in 1980. It tries to take into account, for example, the measurement classifications by Nair and Frank (1980). The countries included here are those in the Price Waterhouse surveys of 1973 and 1975/6, except for the following omissions:

1 Pakistan and India are omitted because of the contradictory evidence of the research about which group they belong to (see Table 6.6). This is coupled with a reluctance to put them with South American or European systems because of developmental reasons and David and Brierley's second criterion (see Chapter 3).
2 Ethiopia and Iran were omitted because of the uncertain nature of their political, social and economic conditions.
3 Greece was omitted because it was not in the 1973 survey and because it did not seem to fit with the groups tentatively suggested by the research.
4 Panama was omitted because of the conflicting results of the writer's research and that of Nair and Frank (1973).
5 Zaire was omitted because it was not in the 1973 survey and because, although it had been a Belgian colony, it seemed out of place with the continental European group.
6 Denmark and Norway were omitted because they did not appear in the 1973 survey, and because it is not clear in which part of the 'macro' group to put them. Table 6.5 would suggest that they should be put with Sweden, which seems eminently sensible on a geographical and cultural basis.

To a large extent, these omissions are due to lack of knowledge (which inspires caution) rather than a weakness in the method of classification. With these nine omissions and the 37 countries contained in the figure, the 46 countries of the 1975/6 survey are accounted for.

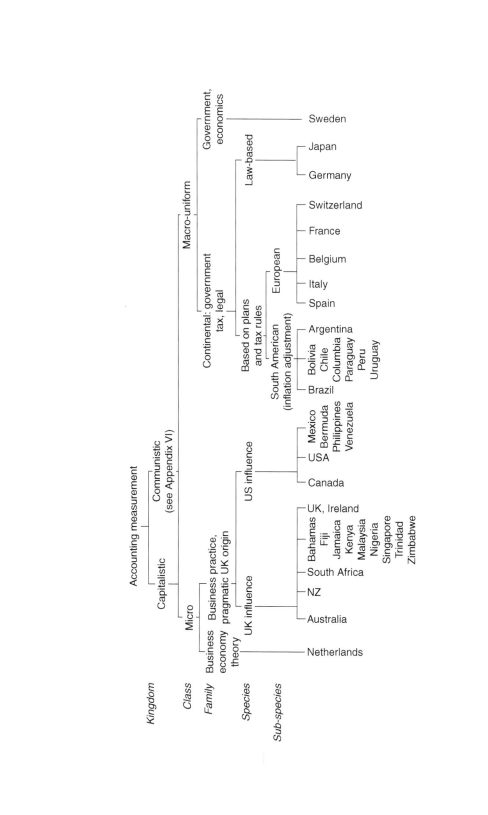

Appendix III

Details of the sample used in Chapter 8

The countries included in our sample are Australia (AU), United Kingdom (UK), Canada (CA), China (CN), Hong Kong (HK), France (FR), Spain (ES), Italy (IT), Germany (DE), Switzerland (CH), South Africa (ZA) and South Korea (SK). The sample comprises the constituents of the major stock market index of the respective country on 31 December 2005 or 31 December 2010 or both.[1] The indexes are: S&P/ASX-50 (AU), FTSE-100 (UK), S&P/TSX-60 (CA), CAC-40 (FR), IBEX-35 (ES), FTSE/MIB-40 (IT), DAX-30 and ten largest (by market capitalisation) constituents of MDAX-50 (DE), SMI (CH), Hang Seng China Enterprises Index (CN), Hang Seng (HK), FTSE/JSE Top 40 (ZA) and KOSPI-50 (SK). The sum of the index constituents is 688.

We exclude certain companies in order to ensure that the national samples are not affected by foreign influence and that we have independent observations. Hence we exclude foreign companies (e.g. Telecom New Zealand in Australia), subsidiaries of listed foreign companies (e.g. TUI Travel in the United Kingdom, which is a subsidiary of the German TUI), Hong Kong companies with a Chinese ultimate parent, i.e. if the ultimate holding company is a Chinese state-owned enterprise (e.g. China Mobile), companies with other foreign influence, i.e. if the company either has a dual-listed structure (e.g. BHP Billiton, which is listed in Australia and the United Kingdom) or has a headquarters abroad (e.g. Royal Dutch Shell in the United Kingdom, which has its headquarters in the Netherlands), and subsidiaries of listed domestic companies already included in the sample (e.g. Enel Green Power in Italy, which is a subsidiary of Enel). The necessary ownership data are hand-collected and we do not simply look at ownership percentages in order to determine whether or not a company is a subsidiary; for example, Saipem in Italy is a subsidiary of Eni although Eni holds substantially less than half of the share capital and voting rights. This results in the exclusion of 102 companies.

We study 2011 IFRS financial statements. The one exception to this is that we include the first available IFRS financial statements for ten Canadian and four South Korean companies having year-ends other than 31 December 2011. However, there are no such reports for some index companies: first, 16 companies (mostly from Canada and Switzerland) use US GAAP and are therefore not considered; second, six Chinese companies use Chinese GAAP only; third, three Canadian companies with rate-regulated activities use Canadian GAAP; fourth, 47 companies were index constituents in 2005 and/or 2010 but had been taken over/delisted by 2011. Consequently, our final sample consists of 514 unique companies (see Table 8.2 for a breakdown by country). For all these companies, with the exception of some South Korean ones, we used English language reports. For those South Korean companies which did not provide consolidated statements in English, we used the information that we could find from regulatory filings (from the 'DART') or from unconsolidated statements.

Note

1 For Canada and South Korea, the two countries where IFRS was not used in 2005, we only include the index constituents on 31 December 2010.

Appendix IV

Data collection and coding procedures for Chapter 8

This appendix provides details on how we collected the data on observable IFRS policy choices (see Table 8.3) and on how we coded the data in order to generate binary choice data (see Table 8.4).

General procedures

Our default procedure is to record the IFRS policy choices based on the information provided in the financial statements or the accounting policies section of the notes. If there is no or insufficient information, other parts of the notes are searched for the relevant information. We ignore cases without a corresponding number in the current year; this applies when a company states a policy choice which was previously made but is not applicable any more. We also ignore choices that only relate to an associate or joint venture.

Specific procedures

Topic 1 (income statement format): 'neither' is recorded if the income statement contains both a by-nature and a by-function expense or if the income statement contains so few lines that it is unclear whether it is 'by nature' or 'by function'. We define a binary choice by distinguishing whether or not the income statement is by nature because the 'neither' cases are usually more similar to 'by function' than 'by nature'. For financial companies, this topic is omitted because the distinction between 'by nature' and 'by function' is not applicable to most of them.

Topic 2 (operating profit shown or not): for financial companies, this topic is omitted because for many of them there is only a line for earnings before taxation (EBT) since EBT = operating profit.

Topic 3 (position of equity profits in the income statement): we define a binary choice by distinguishing whether or not the item is included in operating profit, which we consider to be the key issue. Many financial companies do not have a clear 'operating' or 'financing' section in the income statement; for these, we record that equity profits are *not* included in 'operating' if they are clearly separately shown below the operating expenses items. We ignore cases where both options are used (which applies to two companies).

Topic 4 (balance sheet showing net assets or not): showing 'net current assets' is treated as showing 'net assets'.

Topic 5 (liquidity order of the balance sheet): no specific procedures.

Topic 6 (direct or indirect operating cash flow): information is collected from the cash flow statement only. Otherwise most companies would use indirect cash flows because those using direct cash flows usually show a reconciliation of an income statement number to cash flow from operating activities in the notes.

Topic 7 (position of dividends received in the cash flow statement): we ignore cases where both options are used for different types of dividends (which applies to nine companies).

Topic 8 (position of interest paid in the cash flow statement): our assumption is that companies have interest paid, unless there is evidence against it. Therefore if a company uses the indirect method and the cash flow statement does not show interest paid, it can be inferred that interest paid is included in operating cash flows. Interest paid includes capitalised borrowing costs. We ignore cases where both options are used (which applies to four companies). For financial companies, this topic is omitted because IAS 7.33 states that interest paid is 'usually' classified as operating cash flows for a financial institution.

Topic 9 (some property at fair value or not): only annual revaluations to fair value are considered, not initial recognition, impairments or first-time adoption of IFRS.

Topic 10 (investment property at fair value or not): the choice of valuing some investment property at fair value according to IAS 40.32A is ignored if a company generally uses the cost model.

Topic 11 (some designation of financial instruments at fair value or not): some fair value designation is only recorded if a company clearly states that financial instruments have been designated as at FVTPL (i.e. the fair value option is used) and the notes show a corresponding number to confirm this. The latter is necessary because many companies have boilerplate notes concerning fair value designation even though there is no such designation in the particular company. For financial companies, this topic is omitted because many have some fair value designation due to having a large number of financial instruments.

Topic 12 (inventory valuation): any method other than FIFO or weighted average is ignored. This mainly applies to the 'retail method' used in the retail sector.

For financial companies, this topic is omitted because most of them do not report inventories.

Topic 13 (treatment of actuarial gains/losses): any choice that results in unrecognised actuarial gains and losses (AGL) is treated as using the corridor method, because the key difference between the corridor method and the other options is the existence of unrecognised AGL. We define a binary choice by combining the options 'corridor method' and 'to income in full' because we consider the key issue to be whether or not AGL are ever charged in the income statement, which is not the case under 'actuarial gains and losses to OCI'.

Topic 14 (treatment of joint ventures): the choice of designation as at fair value through profit or loss upon initial recognition (IAS 31.1) is ignored. This only applies to two financial companies in our sample. We ignore the choice of one financial company which uses both proportionate consolidation and the equity method.

References

AAA (1977) 'American Accounting Association 1975–1976: Committee on international accounting operations and education', *Accounting Review*, 52(Supplement), 65–132.

AICPA (2010) *Accounting Trends and Techniques*, Jersey City, NJ: American Institute of Certified Public Accountants

Aldersley-Williams, H. (2011) *Periodic Tales: The Curious Lives of the Elements*, London: Viking.

Alexander, D. and Archer, S. (2000) 'On the myth of "Anglo-Saxon" financial accounting', *International Journal of Accounting*, 35(4), 539–557.

Alexander, D. and Archer, S. (2003) *European Accounting Guide*, New York: Aspen.

Ali, A. and Hwang, L.-S. (2000) 'Country-specific factors related to financial reporting and the value relevance of accounting data', *Journal of Accounting Research*, 38(1), 1–21.

Almond, G.A. (1966) *Comparative Politics Today*, Boston, MA: Little, Brown & Co.

ARC (2005) See the 'Draft Summary Record' of the meeting of ARC on 30 November 2005 at http://ec.europa.eu/internal_market/accounting/docs/arc.

Ball, R. (2006) 'International Financial Reporting Standards (IFRS): pros and cons for investors', *Accounting and Business Research*, 36 (International Accounting Policy Forum), 5–27.

Ball, R.S., Kothari, S.P. and Robin, A. (2000) 'The effect of international institutional factors on properties of accounting earnings', *Journal of Accounting and Economics*, 29(1), 1–51.

Barniv, R., Myring, M.J. and Thomas, W.B. (2005) 'The association between the legal and financial reporting environments and forecast performance of individual analysts', *Contemporary Accounting Research*, 22(4), 727–758.

Basri, G. and Brown, M.E. (2006) 'Planetesimals to brown dwarfs: what is a planet?' *Annual Review of Earth and Planetary Sciences*, 34, 193–216.

Baydoun, N. and Willett, R. (1995) 'Cultural relevance of western accounting systems to developing countries', *Abacus*, 31(1), 67–92.

Beaver, W.H. (1989) *Financial Reporting: An Accounting Revolution* (2nd edn), Englewood Cliffs, NJ: Prentice Hall.

Belkaoui, A. (1995) *International Accounting*, Westport, CT: Quorum Press.

Benston, G.J., Bromwich, M., Litan, R.E. and Wagenhofer, A. (2006) *Worldwide Financial Reporting*, Oxford: Oxford University Press.

Berry, I. (1987) 'The need to classify worldwide accountancy practices', *Accountancy*, 100(October), 90–91.

Bloomfield, L. (1935) 'Linguistic aspects of science', *Philosophy of Science*, 2(4), 499–517.

Bloor, D. (1982) 'Durkheim and Mauss revisited: classification and the sociology of knowledge', *Studies in History and Philosophy of Science*, 13(4), 267–297.

Botosan, C.A. (1997) 'Disclosure level and the cost of equity capital', *Accounting Review*, 72(3), 323–349.

Botzem, S. and Quack, S. (2009) '(No) limits to Anglo-American accounting? Reconstructing the history of the International Accounting Standards Committee: a review article', *Accounting, Organizations and Society*, 34(8), 988–998.

Bowker, G.C. and Star, S.L. (2000) *Sorting Things Out: Classification and its Consequences*, Cambridge, MA: MIT Press.

Briston, R.J. (1978) 'The evolution of accounting in developing countries', *International Journal of Accounting*, 14(1), 105–120.

Briston, R.J. and Liang, F.S. (1990) 'The evolution of corporate reporting in Singapore', *Research in Third World Accounting*, 1, 263–280.

Brotton, J. (2012) *A History of the World in Twelve Maps*, London: Penguin.

Buckley, J.W. and Buckley, M.H. (1974) *The Accounting Profession*, Los Angeles, CA: Melville.

Cable, J. (1985) 'Capital market information and industrial performance: the role of West German banks', *Economic Journal*, 95(1), 118–132.

Cairns, D. (1997) 'The future shape of harmonization: a reply', *European Accounting Review*, 6(2), 305–348.

Camfferman, K. and Zeff, S. (2007) *Financial Reporting and Global Capital Markets: A History of the International Accounting Standards Committee, 1973–2000*, Oxford: Oxford University Press.

CESR (2007) 'CESR work to date in relation to the European Commission's measures on the use of third countries' GAAP in the EU', ref. 07-022b, Committee of European Securities Regulators, April.

Choi, F. and Meek, G. (2005) *International Accounting*, Englewood Cliffs, NJ: Prentice Hall.

Choi, F.D.S. and Mueller, G.G. (1978) *An Introduction to Multinational Accounting*, Englewood Cliffs, NJ: Prentice Hall.

Choi, F.D.S. and Mueller, G.G. (1992) *International Accounting* (2nd edn), Englewood Cliffs, NJ: Prentice Hall.

Chow, L.M., Chau, G.K. and Gray, S.J. (1995) 'Accounting reforms in China: cultural constraints on implementation and development', *Accounting and Business Research*, 26(1), 29–49.

Christensen, H.B. and Nikolaev, V.V. (2013) 'Does fair value accounting for non-financial assets pass the market test?' *Review of Accounting Studies*, 18(3), 734–775.

Christie, A.A. (1990) 'Aggregation of test statistics: an evaluation of the evidence on contracting and size hypotheses', *Journal of Accounting and Economics*, 12(1–3), 15–36.

Clark, P. (1994) *European Financial Reporting: Luxembourg*, London: Routledge.

Cooke, T.E. and Wallace, R.S.O. (1990) 'Financial disclosure regulation and its environment: a review and further analysis', *Journal of Accounting and Public Policy*, 9(2), 79–110.

Coomber, R.R. (1956) 'Hugh Oldcastle and John Mellis', in A.C. Littleton and B.S. Yamey (eds), *Studies in the History of Accounting* (206–214), Homewood, IL: Irwin.

Cormack, R.M. (1971) 'A review of classification', *Journal of the Royal Statistical Society. Series A (General)*, 134(3), 321–367.

d'Arcy, A. (2001) 'Accounting classification and the international harmonisation debate: an empirical investigation', *Accounting, Organizations and Society*, 26(4), 327–349.

d'Arcy, A. (2004) 'Accounting classification and the international debate: a reply to a comment', *Accounting, Organizations and Society*, 29(2), 201–206.

da Costa, R.C., Bourgeois, J.C. and Lawson, W.M. (1978) 'A classification of international financial accounting practices', *International Journal of Accounting*, 13(2), 73–85.

David, R. and Brierley, J.E.C. (1978) *Major Legal Systems in the World Today*, London: Stevens.

David, R. and Brierley, J.E.C. (1985) *Major Legal Systems in the World Today: An Introduction to the Comparative Study of Law* (3rd edn), London: Stevens.

Davidson, R.A., Gelardi, A.M.G. and Li, F. (1996) 'Analysis of the conceptual framework of China's new accounting system', *Accounting Horizons*, 10(1), 58–74.

Deloitte (2006) *China's New Accounting Standards*, London: Deloitte Touche Tohmatsu.

Doupnik, T. and Perera, H. (2009) *International Accounting*, New York: McGraw-Hill.

Doupnik, T.S. and Salter, S.B. (1993) 'An empirical test of a judgemental international classification of financial reporting practices', *Journal of International Business Studies*, 24(1), 41–60.

Doupnik, T.S. and Salter, S.B. (1995) 'External environment, culture, and accounting practice: a preliminary test of a general model of international accounting development', *International Journal of Accounting*, 30(3), 189–207.

Dow, D. and Karunaratna, A. (2006) 'Developing a multidimensional instrument to measure physic distance stimuli', *Journal of International Business Studies*, 37(5), 578–602.

Duff, R.J. and Nickrent, D.L. (1999) 'Phylogenetic relationships of land plants using mitochondrial small-subunit rDNA sequences', *American Journal of Botany*, 86(3), 372–386.

Durkheim, E. and Mauss, M. (1903) 'De quelques formes primitives de classification: contribution à l'étude des représentations collectives', *L'Année Sociologique*, 6(1901–1902), 1–72. As translated in R. Needham (1963) *Primitive Classification*, London: Cohen and West.

Egger, M., Smith, G.D. and Phillips, A.N. (1997) 'Meta-analysis: principles and procedures', *BMJ*, 315(7121), 1533–1537.

Evans, L. (2004) 'Language translation and the problem of international communication', *Accounting, Auditing and Accountability Journal*, 17(2), 210–248.

FEE (2005) *Reference to the Financial Reporting Framework in the EU in Accounting Policies and in the Audit Report and Applicability of Endorsed IFRS*, Brussels: Fédération des Experts Comptables Européens.

Finer, S.E. (1970) *Comparative Government*, London: Penguin.

Foucault, M. (1970) *The Order of Things: An Archaeology of the Human Sciences*, London: Tavistock.

Frank, W.G. (1979) 'An empirical analysis of international accounting principles', *Journal of Accounting Research*, 17(2), 593–605.

Franks, J. and Mayer, C. (1992) 'Corporate control: a synthesis of the international evidence', Working Paper of London Business School and University of Warwick.

Gambling, T. and Abdel-Karim, R.A.A. (1991) *Business and Accounting Ethics in Islam*, London: Mansell.

Gernon, H. and Wallace, R.S.O. (1995) 'International accounting research: a review of its ecology, contending theories and methodologies', *Journal of Accounting Literature*, 14, 54–106.

Gonzalo, J.A. and Gallizo, J.L. (1992) *European Financial Reporting: Spain*, London: Routledge.

Goodrich, P.S. (1982) 'A typology of international accounting principles and policies', *AUTA Review*, 14(1), 37–61.

Goodrich, P.S. (1983) 'A typology of international accounting principles and policies: a reply to a comment', *AUTA Review*, 15(1), 53–56.

Gordon, A.D. (1981) *Classification Methods for the Exploratory Analysis of Multivariate Data*, London: Chapman and Hall.

Gray, S.J. (1988) 'Towards a theory of cultural influence on the development of accounting systems internationally', *Abacus*, 24(1), 1–15.

Green, R.E., Krause, J. and 54 other authors (2010) 'A draft sequence of the Neandertal genome', *Science*, 328(5979), 710–722.

Gregory, P.R. and Stuart, R.C. (1980) *Comparative Economic Systems*, Boston, MA: Houghton Mifflin.

Gregory, P.R. and Stuart, R.C. (2003) *Comparing Economic Systems in the Twenty-first Century*, Independence, KS: Cengage Learning.

Guenther, D.A. and Young, D. (2000) 'The association between financial accounting measures and real economic activity: a multinational study', *Journal of Accounting and Economics*, 29(1), 53–72.

Haller, A. and Eierle, B. (2004) 'The adaptation of German accounting rules to IFRS: a legislative balancing act', *Accounting in Europe*, 1, 27–50.

Hamid, S.R., Craig, R. and Clarke, F.L. (1993) 'Religion: a confounding cultural element in the international harmonization of accounting?' *Abacus*, 29(2), 131–148.

Harrison, G.L. and McKinnon, J.L. (1986) 'Culture and accounting change: a new perspective on corporate reporting regulation and accounting policy formulation', *Accounting, Organizations and Society*, 11(3), 233–252.

Hatfield, H.R. (1911) 'Some variations in accounting practice in England, France, Germany and the United States', reprinted in 1966 in *Journal of Accounting Research*, 4(2), 169–182.

Hennes, M. and Metzger, S. (2010) 'Der unbekannte Feind aus London', *Handelsblatt*, 21 September, 18. Retrieved 15 April 2013, from www.handelsblatt.com/unternehmen/management/strategie/iasb-bilanzierungsregeln-der-unbekannte-feind-aus-london/3629726.html.

Hofstede, G. (1980) *Culture's Consequences: International Differences in Work-related Values*, Beverly Hills, CA: Sage Publications.

Hope, O.K. (2003) 'Disclosure practices, enforcement of accounting standards, and analysts' forecast accuracy: an international study', *Journal of Accounting Research*, 41(2), 235–272.

Hove, M.R. (1986) 'Accounting practices in developing countries: colonialism's legacy of inappropriate technologies', *International Journal of Accounting*, 22(1), 81–100.

Hung, M. (2000) 'Accounting standards and value relevance of financial statements: an international analysis', *Journal of Accounting and Economics*, 30(3), 401–420.

Hutcheson, G. and Sofroniou, N. (1999) *The Multivariate Social Scientist: Introductory Statistics using Generalized Linear Models*, Thousand Oaks, CA: Sage Publications.

IAU (2006) 'International Astronomical Union 2006 General Assembly: resolution B5: definition of a planet in the solar system, resolution B6: Pluto'. Retrieved 15 April 2013, from www.iau.org/static/resolutions/Resolution_GA26-5-6.pdf.

Jaafar, A. and McLeay, S. (2007) 'Country effects and sector effects on the harmonization of accounting policy choice', *Abacus*, 43(2), 156–189.

Jeanjean, T., Lesage, C. and Stolowy, H. (2010) 'Why do you speak English (in your annual report)?' *International Journal of Accounting*, 45(2), 200–223.

Jensen, M.C. and Meckling, W.H. (1976) 'Theory of the firm: managerial behavior, agency costs, and ownership structure', *Journal of Financial Economics*, 3, 305–360.

Kagan, K.K. (1955) *Three Great Systems of Jurisprudence*, London: Stevens.

Kaiser, H.F. (1970) 'A second generation little jiffy', *Psychometrika*, 35(4), 401–415.

Kaiser, H.F. (1974) 'An index of factorial simplicity', *Psychometrika*, 39(1), 31–36.

Kim, J.-O. and Mueller, C.W. (1978) *Introduction to Factor Analysis: What It Is and How to Do It* (Quantitative Applications in the Social Sciences Series, No. 13), Thousand Oaks, CA: Sage.

Kirsch, R.J. (2006) *The International Accounting Standards Committee: A Political History*, Kingston-upon-Thames: Wolters Kluwer.

Kleekämper, H. (2000) 'IASC: das Trojanische Pferd der SEC?' in W. Ballwieser (ed.), *US-amerikanische Rechnungslegung: Grundlagen und Vergleiche mit deutschem Recht* (4th edn, 467–484), Stuttgart: Schäffer-Poeschel.

Kvaal, E. and Nobes, C.W. (2010) 'International differences in IFRS policy choice: a research note', *Accounting and Business Research*, 40(2), 173–187.

Kvaal, E. and Nobes, C.W. (2012) 'IFRS policy changes and the continuation of national patterns of IFRS practice', *European Accounting Review*, 21(2), 343–371.

La Porta, R., Lopez-de-Silanes, F., Shleifer, A. and Vishny, R.W. (1997) 'Legal determinants of external finance', *Journal of Finance*, 52(3), 1131–1150.

La Porta, R., Lopez-de-Silanes, F., Shleifer, A. and Vishny, R.W. (1998) 'Law and finance', *Journal of Political Economy*, 106(6), 1113–1154.

Lamb, M. (1995) 'When is a group a group? Convergence of concepts of "group" in European Union corporation tax', *European Accounting Review*, 4(1), 33–78.

Lamb, M., Nobes, C.W. and Roberts, A.D. (1998) 'International variations in the connections between tax and financial reporting', *Accounting and Business Research*, 28(3), 173–188.

Leuz, C. (2010) 'Different approaches to corporate reporting regulation: how jurisdictions differ and why', *Accounting and Business Research* (International Accounting Policy Forum), 40(3), 229–256.

Leuz, C., Nanda, D. and Wysocki, P.D. (2003) 'Earnings management and investor protection: an international comparison', *Journal of Financial Economics*, 69(3), 505–527.

Lev, B. and Nissim, D. (2004) 'Taxable income, future earnings, and equity values', *Accounting Review*, 79, 1039–1074.

Linnaeus, C. (1751) 'Philosophia botanica', in S. Freer (tr.), *Linnaeus' Philosophia Botanica*, Oxford: Oxford University Press (2003).

Lovejoy, A.O. (1964) *The Great Chain of Being: A Study of the History of an Idea*, Cambridge, MA: Harvard University Press.

Meek, G.K. and Saudagaran, S.M. (1990) 'A survey of research on financial reporting in a transnational context', *Journal of Accounting Literature*, 9, 145–182.

Miller, M.C. (1994) 'Australia', in T.E. Cooke and R.H. Parker (eds), *Financial Reporting in the West Pacific Rim* (ch. 10), London: Routledge.

Mishler, B.D. (2009) 'Three centuries of paradigm changes in biological classification: is the end in sight?' *Taxon*, 58(1), 61–67.

Mueller, G.G. (1967) *International Accounting*, Part I, New York: Macmillan.

Mueller, G.G. (1968) 'Accounting principles generally accepted in the United States versus those generally accepted elsewhere', *International Journal of Accounting*, 3(1), 91–103.

Nair, R.D. and Frank, W.G. (1980) 'The impact of disclosure and measurement practices on international accounting classifications', *Accounting Review*, 55(3), 426–450.

Neuberger, E. and Duffy, W.J. (1976) *Comparative Economic Systems: A Decision-making Approach*, Boston, MA: Allyn and Bacon.

Nie, N., Bent, D. and Hadlai Hull, C. (1974) *Statistical Package for the Social Sciences*, New York: McGraw Hill.

Nobes, C.W. (1981) 'An empirical analysis of international accounting principles: a comment', *Journal of Accounting Research*, 19(Spring), 268–270.

Nobes, C.W. (1983a) 'A typology of international accounting principles and policies: a reply to a reply', *AUTA Review*, 15(1), 56–58.

Nobes, C.W. (1983b) 'A judgmental international classification of financial reporting practices', *Journal of Business Finance and Accounting*, 10(1), 1–19.

Nobes, C.W. (1984) *International Classification of Financial Reporting*, London: Croom Helm.

Nobes, C.W. (1988) 'The causes of financial reporting differences', in C.W. Nobes and R.H. Parker (eds), *Issues in Multinational Accounting* (ch. 2), Oxford: Philip Allan.

Nobes, C.W. (1992a) 'Classification of accounting systems using competencies as a dis-criminating variable: a comment', *Journal of Business Finance and Accounting*, 19(1), 153–155.

Nobes, C.W. (1992b) *International Classification of Financial Reporting* (2nd edn), London: Routledge.

Nobes, C.W. (1992c) *Accounting Comparisons: UK/Europe*, III, London: Gee & Co.

Nobes, C.W. (1992d) *Accounting Comparisons: UK/Europe*, IV, London: Gee & Co.

Nobes, C.W. (1992e) *Accounting Comparisons: UK/Europe*, V, London: Gee & Co.

Nobes, C.W. (1996) 'The effects of international differences in the tax treatment of good-will: a comment', *Journal of International Business Studies*, 27(3), 589–592.

Nobes, C.W. (1998) 'Towards a general model of the reasons for international differences in financial reporting', *Abacus*, 34(2), 162–187.

Nobes, C.W. (2003) 'On the myth of "Anglo-Saxon" accounting: a comment', *International Journal of Accounting*, 38(1), 95–104.

Nobes, C.W. (2004) 'On accounting classification and the international harmonisation debate', *Accounting, Organizations and Society*, 29(2), 189–200.

Nobes, C.W. (2006) 'The survival of international differences under IFRS: towards a research agenda', *Accounting and Business Research*, 36(3), 233–245.

Nobes, C.W. (2008) 'Accounting classification in the IFRS era', *Australian Accounting Review*, 18(3), 191–198.

Nobes, C.W. (2011) 'IFRS practices and the persistence of accounting system classifica-tion', *Abacus*, 47(3), 267–283.

Nobes, C.W. (2013) 'The continued survival of international differences under IFRS', *Accounting and Business Research*, 43(2), 83–111.

Nobes, C.W. and Parker, R.H. (1995) *Comparative International Accounting* (4th edn), Harlow: Prentice Hall.

Nobes, C.W. and Parker, R.H. (2004) *Comparative International Accounting* (8th edn), Harlow: Prentice Hall.

Nobes, C.W. and Parker, R.H. (2012) *Comparative International Accounting* (12th edn), Harlow: Prentice Hall.

Nobes, C.W. and Perramon, J. (2013) 'Firm size and national profiles of IFRS policy choice', *Australian Accounting Review*, 23(3), 208–215.

Nobes, C.W. and Roberts, A.D. (2000) 'Towards a unifying model of systems of law, corporate financing, accounting and corporate governance', *Australian Accounting Review*, 10(1), 26–34.

Nobes, C.W. and Schwencke, H.R. (2006) 'Modelling the links between tax and financial reporting: a longitudinal examination of Norway over 30 years up to IFRS adoption', *European Accounting Review*, 15(1), 63–87.

Nobes, C.W. and Stadler, C. (2013) 'How arbitrary are international accounting classifications? Lessons from centuries of classifying in many disciplines, and experiments with IFRS data', *Accounting, Organizations and Society*, 38(8), 573–595.

Nobes, C.W. and Zeff, S.A. (2008) 'Auditor affirmations of compliance with IFRS around the world: an exploratory study', *Accounting Perspectives*, 7(4), 279–292.

O'Donnell, E. and Prather-Kinsey, J. (2010) 'Nationality and differences in auditor risk assessment: a research note with experimental evidence', *Accounting, Organizations and Society*, 35(5), 558–564.

Ordelheide, D. and KPMG (1995) *Transnational Accounting*, London: Macmillan.

Ordelheide, D. and KPMG (2001) *Transnational Accounting* (2nd edn), Basingstoke: Palgrave.

Ordelheide, D. and Semler, A. (1995) 'A reference matrix', in D. Ordelheide and KPMG (eds), *Transnational Accounting (TRANSACC)* (1–67), London: Macmillan.

Parker, R.H. (1989) 'Importing and exporting accounting: the British experience', in Hopwood, A.G. (ed.), *International Pressures for Accounting Change* (7–29), Harlow: Prentice Hall.

Parker, R.H. (1991) 'Financial reporting in the Netherlands', in C.W. Nobes and R.H. Parker (eds), *Comparative International Accounting* (3rd edn, ch. 10), Harlow: Prentice Hall.

Parry, M. and Grove, R. (1990) 'Does training more accountants raise the standards of accounting in third world countries? A study of Bangladesh', *Research in Third World Accounting*, 1, 3–54.

Perec, G. (1985) *Penser/classer*, Rungis: Hachette.

Previts, G.J. (1975) 'On the subject of methodology and models for international accountancy', *International Journal of Accounting*, Spring, 1–12.

Price Waterhouse (1973) *Accounting Principles and Reporting Practices: A Survey in 38 Countries*, New York: Price Waterhouse.

Price Waterhouse (1976) *A Survey in 46 Countries: Accounting Principles and Reporting Practices*, London: Institute of Chartered Accountants in England and Wales.

Price Waterhouse (1979) *International Survey of Accounting Principles and Reporting Practices*, Scarborough, ON: Butterworths

Puxty, A.G., Willmott, H.C., Cooper, D.J. and Lowe, T. (1987) 'Modes of regulation in advanced capitalism: locating accountancy in four countries', *Accounting, Organizations and Society*, 12(3), 273–291.

Radebaugh, L.H. (1975) 'Environmental factors influencing the development of accounting objectives, standards and practices in Peru', *International Journal of Accounting*, 11(1), 39–56.

Radebaugh, L.H. and Gray, S.J. (1993) *International Accounting and Multinational Enterprises*, New York: Wiley.

Radebaugh, L.H., Gray, S.J. and Black, E.L. (2006) *International Accounting and Multinational Enterprises*, New York: Wiley.

Rahman, A., Perera, H. and Ganeshanandam, S. (1996) 'Measurement of formal harmonisation in accounting: an exploratory study', *Accounting and Business Research*, 26(4), 325–339.

Roberts, A. (1995) 'The very idea of classification in international accounting', *Accounting, Organizations and Society*, 20(7–8), 639–664.

Roberts, C., Weetman, P. and Gordon, P. (2008) *International Corporate Reporting: A Comparative Approach*, Harlow: Prentice Hall.

Ruhlen, M. (1991) *A Guide to the World's Languages, Vol. 1: Classification*, Stanford, CA: Stanford University Press.

Schweikart, J.A. (1985) 'Contingency theory as a framework for research in international accounting', *International Journal of Accounting*, 21(1), 89–98.

Seidler, L.J. (1967) 'International accounting: the ultimate theory course', *Accounting Review*, 42(4), 775–781.

Shils, E. (1966) *Political Development in the New States*, The Hague: Mouton.

Shoenthal, E.R. (1989) 'Classification of accounting systems using competencies as a discriminating variable: a Great Britain–United States study', *Journal of Business Finance and Accounting*, 16(4), 549–563.

Soeters, J. and Schreuder, H. (1988) 'The interaction between national and organizational cultures in accounting firms', *Accounting, Organizations and Society*, 13(1), 75–85.

Standish, P. (1990) 'Origins of the Plan Comptable Général: a study in cultural intrusion and reaction', *Accounting and Business Research*, 20(80), 337–351.

Standish, P.E.M. (1995) 'Financial reporting in France', in C.W. Nobes and R.H. Parker (eds), *Comparative International Accounting* (4th edn, ch. 11), Harlow: Prentice Hall.

Standish, P.E.M. (2000) 'Financial reporting in France', in C.W. Nobes and R.H. Parker (eds.), *Comparative International Accounting* (181–225), Harlow: Prentice Hall.

Steiper, M.E. and Young, N.M. (2006) 'Primate molecular divergence dates', *Molecular Phylogenetics and Evolution*, 41(2), 384–394.

Stringer, C. (2011) *The Origin of Our Species*, London: Penguin.

Tarca, A., Morris, R.D. and Moy, M. (2012) 'An investigation of the relationship between use of International Accounting Standards and source of company finance in Germany', *Abacus*, 49(1), 74–98.

Thomson, A. (2009) 'Comment: Australia's adoption of IFRSs: a clarification from the AASB', *Australian Accounting Review*, 19(2), 153.

Tweedie, D.P. and Whittington, G. (1984) *The Debate on Inflation Accounting*, Cambridge: Cambridge University Press.

Wallace, R.S.O. and Gernon, H. (1991) 'Frameworks for international comparative accounting', *Journal of Accounting Literature*, 10, 209–264.

Walton, P., Haller, A. and Raffournier, B. (2003) *International Accounting*, London: Thomson.

Watts, R.L. and Zimmerman, J.L. (1979) 'The demand for and supply of accounting theories: the market for excuses', *Accounting Review*, 54(2), 273–305.

Wehrfritz, M., Haller, A. and Walton, P. (2012) 'National influence on the application of IFRS: interpretations and accounting estimates by German and British accountants', Working Paper, University of Regensburg.

Whittington, G. (2005) 'The adoption of international accounting standards in the European Union', *European Accounting Review*, 14(1), 127–153.

Wildman, D.E., Uddin, M., Liu, G., Grossman, L.I. and Goodman, M. (2003) 'Implications of natural selection in shaping 99.4% nonsynonymous DNA identity between humans and chimpanzees: enlarging genus Homo', *Proceedings of the National Academy of Sciences of the United States of America*, 100(12), 7181–7188.

Xiao, J.Z., Weetman, P. and Sun, M. (2004) 'Political influence and co-existence of a uniform accounting system and accounting standards: recent developments in China', *Abacus*, 40(2), 193–218.

Yamey, B. (1997) 'Diversity in mercantile accounting in Western Europe, 1300–1800', in T.E. Cooke and C.W. Nobes (eds), *The Development of Accounting in an International Context* (12–29), London: Routledge.

Zeff, S.A. (1979) *Forging Accounting Principles in New Zealand*, Wellington: Victoria University Press.

Zeff, S.A. (2010) 'Political lobbying on accounting standards: US, UK and international experience', in C.W. Nobes and R.H. Parker (eds), *Comparative International Accounting* (ch. 11), Harlow: Prentice Hall.

Zeff, S.A. and Nobes, C.W. (2010) 'Has Australia (or any other jurisdiction) "adopted" IFRS?' *Australian Accounting Review*, 20(2), 178–184.

Zeff, S.A., van der Wel, F. and Camfferman, K. (1992) *Company Financial Reporting: A Historical and Comparative Study of the Dutch Regulatory Process*, Amsterdam: North-Holland.

Zysman, J. (1983) *Government, Markets and Growth: Financial Systems and the Politics of Industrial Change*, Ithaca, NY: Cornell University Press and Oxford: Martin Robertson.

Index

Page numbers in *italics* denote tables, those in **bold** denote figures.